I0831248

New Readings in British Drama

Mesut Günenç and Enes Kavak (eds.)

New Readings in British Drama

From the Post-War Period to the Contemporary Era

Bibliographic Information published by the Deutsche Nationalbibliothek
The Deutsche Nationalbibliothek lists this publication in the Deutsche Nationalbibliografie; detailed bibliographic data is available online at http://dnb.d-nb.de.

Library of Congress Cataloging-in-Publication Data
A CIP catalog record for this book has been applied for at the Library of Congress.

ISBN 978-3-631-86022-9 (Print)
E-ISBN 978-3-631-86023-6 (E-PDF)
E-ISBN 978-3-631-86586-6 (EPUB)
10.3726/b18947

Peter Lang – Berlin · Bern · Bruxelles · Istanbul · New York · Oxford · Warszawa · Wien

This publication has been peer reviewed.

www.peterlang.com

Contents

Introduction

New Readings in British Drama: From the Post-War Period to the Contemporary Era includes chapters by scholars specializing in drama and theatre studies at various Turkish universities. The book aims to present new readings of British plays produced after the post--Second World War period by underlining the fact that literary theories have never been stagnant and exhausted in the field of drama as part of literary studies. Scholarly editions focusing exclusively on contemporary drama and its critical readings are still a rarity, as contemporary literary scholars tend to neglect drama in favour of fiction. Books and edited volumes such as Oscar G. Brockett's *Perspectives on Contemporary Theatre* (1999), Vicky Angelaki's *Contemporary British Theatre: Breaking New Ground* (2013), Gabriele Griffin's *Contemporary Black and Asian Women Playwrights in Britain* (2003), Cristina Delgado-García's *Rethinking Character in Contemporary British Theatre: Aesthetics, Politics, Subjectivity* (2015), Kara Reilly's *Contemporary Approaches to Adaptation in Theatre* (2018) and Joe Kelleher and Nicholas Ridout's *Contemporary Theatres in Europe: A Critical Companion* (2006) offer important critical insights into different aspects of contemporary British and European theatres and they have all contributed to the field by attracting interest in critical readings. Following these examples, we have decided to offer an edited volume featuring new perspectives into a select collection of British plays written after World War II by emphasizing how key theoretical approaches can help elucidate theatrical texts and their performances from a contemporary critical standpoint.

Literary theory offers an invaluable instrument and critical space for appreciation, signification and repositioning of drama/theatre in the realms of philosophy, culture and politics. In the second half of the twentieth century, postmodernism and post-structuralism became the two most influential movements guiding and inspiring playwrights and directors who confronted and dismantled the dominant political and social discourses of their age. Post-structuralism, most basically, stands for a reaction to structuralism by employing a metalinguistic reading of social and political power relations. The famous philosopher and theorist Michel Foucault asserted that the human subject, who is historically specific, is under the influence of the dominant discourses of a historical period, which builds up the bodies of knowledge and subjectivities. On the contrary, the French sociologist and philosopher, Baudrillard saw culture as completely negated of political and other meanings and associations. He blamed commodification, commercial marketing and mass media for the loss of meaning in contemporary societies. He presented a critique of the dominant modes of thought and the power of technology in his writings on postmodernism and contemporary culture. In this context, playwrights such as Harold Pinter, Edward Albee, Caryl Churchill, Tom Stoppard, Sarah Kane and Mark Ravenhill wrote the best examples of postmodern British plays.

Postcolonial criticism of the British theatre focuses on the theatres that appeared in the immediate post–Second World War period. It offers the critiques of theatrical works on or from the ex-colonies such as India and the Caribbean as well as countries such as Canada, America and England. Postcolonial criticism in theatre, therefore, explores the colonial past and its relation to the current White, Black and mixed communities through dramatic portrayals of individuals and their subjective experiences. However, a group of new Black playwrights such as Roy Williams, Jackie Kay, Kwame Kwei-Armah, debbie tucker green, Winsome Pinnock and Bola Agbaje have brought a new sensibility to the British stage with their plays on contemporary issues of the Black diaspora in the United Kingdom. These plays go beyond the confines of postcolonial tradition and offer us a unique window into the lives and experiences of Black people in multiethnic and multicultural urban centres of British society in the new millennium.

Posthumanism, which was conceptualized around the 1990s, puts forward that an anthropocentric future and its social, political and moral circumstances are longer sustainable and sensible in a technologically and scientifically forward-looking world. It, thus, proposes that it is possible and reasonable for humans to exceed their corporeal and mental boundaries physiologically, politically and philosophically. The progressive mentality of the theory has offered a new critical realm for theatre writers and critics to discover the unexplored aspects of posthuman possibilities and related philosophical disputes in theatre. Plays such as Mark Ravenhill's *Faust Is Dead* (1997), Sarah Kane's *Crave* (1998), Katie Mitchell's *The Waves* (2006), Lucy Prebble's *The Sugar Syndrome* (2003) and Sarah Ruhl's *Dead Man's Cell Phone* (2007) displayed a posthumanist stance in contemporary theatre.

Postdramatic theatre is a theatre of states and dynamic pictorial and performative scenes. It rebuffs the conventional representation of the material world and distorts the linearity of time. Hans-Thies Lehmann, examining the theory of drama, divides periods such as predramatic, dramatic and postdramatic. Analysing avant-garde movements, Bertolt Brecht and Gertrude Stein, Lehmann saw the crises in drama and the total rejection of Aristotle's mimesis as a key aim in contemporary theatre and defended the staging of performative states as aesthetic constructions rather than the narrative representations of life. The traces of postdramatic theatre can be seen in the work of companies such as the Wooster Group in the USA and Forced Entertainment in the UK between the 1970s and 1980s. Playwrights such as Heiner Müller, Martin Crimp, Mark Ravenhill, Sarah Kane, Simon Stephens and Tim Crouch are notable representatives of postdramatic theatre in Europe.

All these post–Second World War theories provided a fertile ground for the critical analyses of dramatic, postdramatic and avant-garde plays written and produced by contemporary British playwrights from new and diverse perspectives. In this respect, each chapter of the book aims to answer the following:

- how the theories of the postwar period are essential to our understanding of contemporary drama and theatrical performances;
- what critical genealogies of the theory are relevant to theatre and its criticism today;
- in what ways these theories offer new insights into contemporary drama, dramaturgy and theatre performances today;
- in what ways key literary theories and discourses subvert previous readings of British drama.

Our contributors recognize that the question for theatre writers and critics today lies precisely in how to pinpoint, conceptualize and examine what is to be qualified/disqualified, essential/non-essential, potential/non-potential and meaningful/empty in contemporary theatre, the productions and scripts of which mostly emerged as a reaction to the notable literary theories of the twentieth century. We have attempted to answer the posed questions by examining the works of Tom Stoppard, Caryl Churchill, Sarah Kane, Roy Williams, Mark Ravenhill, Thomas Eccleshare, Anders Lutsgarten and Jackie Kay from the perspectives of the critical theories. Accordingly, as the scholars working in the field of English Literature and Drama Studies in Turkey, we would like to stress the criticality of literary theories in our valuation and understanding of dramatic works and express our keen interest in drama and theatre criticism, which, we hope, will generate further interest in the field.

The contributions to this study have taken up different perspectives into post–-Second World War theories and offer new critical insights into a select collection of British plays as summarized below.

The first chapter by Mehmet Akif Balkaya helps contextualize Tom Stoppard's play *After Magritte* within the context of post-structuralism. The author aims to show to what extent symbols may not get proper meanings within the post-structuralist nature of the play read through Jacques Derrida, Michel Foucault and Albert Camus's ideas on deconstruction, power relations and existentialism, respectively. Stoppard's play undermines wholeness within the meaning of the text itself; therefore, no final statement of meaning can be established. The chapter, then, discusses the complicated reality perceived by the characters in *After Magritte* by dealing with problems such as reality/misperception, uncertainty/doubt and truth/failure.

In the second chapter, Gül Kurtuluş writes on Caryl Churchill's Theatre and reassesses her place in the contemporary theatrical world through her play *Cloud Nine*, which marks a significant point in the epoch of the postmodern theatre. The author tries to reflect how Churchill's plays are very much compatible with the new theatre forms such as postmodern and contemporary experimental alternatives in the 1970s. The chapter argues that *Cloud Nine* offers a link between postmodernist theory, specifically post-Brechtian theatre, and current theoretical discussions.

In the third chapter, Mesut Günenç examines *Phaedra's Love*, which reflects the tragic side of postdramatic theatre and features a more rapeful and disordered structure than theatrical form. The study analyses one of the most distinctive contemporary British playwrights, Sarah Kane, by drawing on the philosophy of Hans Thies Lehmann's postdramatic theatre and his theory of postdramatic tragedy.

In the fourth chapter, Enes Kavak and Gökçe Akarik contribute the volume with a study on Roy Williams' *The No Boys Cricket Club*, which looks into contemporary Black British theatre with its portrayal of nostalgia and unique Black characters who go through personal crises. The play presents an imaginative quest instigated by nostalgia and existential anxieties of two female Black characters in East London in which the past is envisioned as a liminal space for reclamation and transformation of self away from personal disillusionments and intra-family rifts. The chapter thus examines the Black characters' search for meaning and coherence in the contemporary multicultural society and the theatrical strategies of Black theatre as an offshoot of diaspora literature in the new century.

In the fifth chapter, Mustafa Bal examines Mark Ravenhill's, a distinctive playwright of the new generation of the 1990s, apocalyptic attitude by focusing on his play *Faust Is Dead*. Being the last decade of the second millennium, the 1990s was a period when the apocalyptic discourse found more reflections in western philosophy and literature. With its taboo-breaking, controversial and confrontational aesthetics, the in-yer-face theatre of British literature accorded with the apocalyptic paradigm of the age. After a comprehensive and close analysis of the play, the author ultimately indicates that there is a strong sense of apocalypticism in Ravenhill's *Faust Is Dead*.

In the sixth chapter, Özlem Karadağ hones in on Thomas Eccleshare's *Instructions for Correct Assembly*. Eccleshare's deliberate choice of drawing a thin line between being a humanoid and being a human helps us investigate the waters of the posthuman condition while questioning the anthropocentric and excessively consumerist approach of humanity. Thus, after a brief introduction to posthumanist criticism and with references to academics such as Braidotti, Wolfe and Haraway, this chapter scrutinizes how this play and theatre, a dominantly human-centric art, achieve to convey posthumanism to the audience.

In the seventh chapter, Hakan Gültekin analyses post-neoliberalism in Anders Lustgarten's *If You Don't Let Us Dream, We Won't Let You Sleep*. The impetus behind this study is to discover the dialectical relationship between Lustgarten's play and the society in which the characters live. The author also interrogates how the post-neoliberal age disrupts the initial values of western society and social consent because of the economic and social injustices.

In the final chapter, Pelin Doğan analyses Jackie Kay's *Chiaeoscuro* by focusing on debates and researches pondering about the possibilities of pluralism in critical discourse about British theatre at the turn of the twenty-first century. Unlike liberal or modernist conceptualization of identity, which assumes a universal, coherent and solid essence, the post-structuralist view of identity positions the individual in the intricately woven networks and practices of culture as well as prevailing discourses. Within the framework of the intersectional feminist approach, the chapter explores the multidimensional forms of domination and practices of discrimination that emerge at the intersection of different axes of identity belongings, with particular attention to the playwright's political play *Chiaroscuro*.

Mehmet Akif Balkaya

The Unbearable Absence of Existence: The Post-Structuralist Condition in Tom Stoppard's *After Magritte*

Tom Stoppard's (1937–) *After Magritte* was first performed at the Ambiance Lunch Hour Theatre Club in 1970. The play bears surrealist features in that it is named after the Belgian surrealist painter René Magritte's (1898–1967) style in art, as what seems to be there is not necessarily expressed in the way put forth in art or drama before the surrealist movement. The tension among the characters is to such an extent that any signifier may not get a corresponding signified; therefore, any meaning is deferred and lost in the text. Thus, what seems to be existent is absent, as the text challenges itself through deferment. Each time one supposes that meaning is established, what is thought to be referred to is sucked into a whirlpool within the text. Such are among the reasons that lead absence and existence to be put into a chaos of various anomalies through a supposedly rule-governed text. Misunderstanding, and misinterpretation, thus, dominates the text that thereby becomes meaningless, and disordered. In this context, this chapter aims to study to what extent symbols may not get proper meanings because of the post-structuralist condition of the play. To this end, the chapter works up into an analysis that presents how the relationship between the signifier and the signified remains in between the existence and absence of meaning. Finally, it is put forth that the play deconstructs itself rather than providing a reasonable, understandable meaning.

After Magritte "is a mildly surrealistic farce, which plays with confusions and cross-purposes …, and involves switches between reality and various kinds of illusion …."[1] Stoppard raises the mystery and absurdity of the room through his use of language and description. As for the existence of the mother, he writes: "[s]he could be dead; but is not."[2] The chaos obtained by what anything or anyone seems to be or not is strengthened by the use and repetitions of "but is not" within the text. Mother lies on the ironing board, and a towel covers her. As Holmes watches the Harrisses through the window, the image that he sees is

1 Jonathan Bennett, "Philosophy and Mr. Stoppard," *Philosophy* 50, no. 191 (1975): 5.
2 Tom Stoppard, Tom Stoppard: Plays 1 (London: Faber & Faber, 1996), 49.

supposed to be the clues of amputation. Yet, Mother lies on the ironing board, as she has a backache, and because the bathroom light is to be repaired by Harris. However, this imagery through the window as a signifier signifies and stands for an unsolved crime scene for Foot. Therefore, reality and perceptions clash so many times that no signifier may have a corresponding signified that is true for everyone within the play. The scene is like a crime scene as in René Magritte's *L'assasin Menacé*.

Magritte's painting was first exhibited in Brussels, in 1927. Stoppard takes that painting as a signified to create his text. Regarding the similarity, Anna Suwalska-Kolecka remarks, "[t]he affinity between these two artists can be traced both in the shared philosophical concepts and similar methods of presentation. Magritte believed in a relativist universe following the direction of the subjective perception rather than the hegemony of the received opinion and rejected reason as the means of knowing the reality."[3] Magritte's painting becomes a trace that the text, in a way, pursues. Katherine Kelly has put it,

> The "afterness" or secondariness of Stoppard's play refers … not only to the narrative ordering of events that places the Harris family's appearance on stage after their visit to a Magritte exhibit but also to the playwright's taking after the "perceptual hermeneutics" of Magritte, according to which, in a nutshell, the Harrises are at once the subject and object of a perceptual mirage.[4]

Since the complicated perceptions are perceived as reality by the characters, *After Magritte* deals with such problems as reality/misperception, uncertainty/doubt and truth/failure as represented through the Harrises' "strange" room.

In the painting, however, a corpse lies on a lounge while a man in a suit listens to a gramophone. There are three men outside the window and two men in the doorway. Like the painting, the play opens in such chaos that Holmes and Foot suppose that they are after a crime. Concerning the similarities between the play and the painting, Schmitt remarks,

> In the painting the towel covers only her neck; in the play it covers all but her feet and head, and she wears a bathing cap. In the painting she is young, but not in the play. In the painting two men wear bowler hats; in the play a bowler hat rests on the woman's

---

3 Anna Suwalska-Kolecka, "Tom Stoppard's After Magritte: The World of Uncertainty," *Acta Neophilologica* 3 (2001): 296, https://czasopisma.uwm.edu.pl/index.php/an/article/view/1588.

4 Katherine E. Kelly, "Tom Stoppard's 'Artist Descending a Staircase': Outdoing the 'Dada' Duchamp," *Comparative Drama* 20, no. 3 (1986): 191–92.

stomach. In the painting there is a gramophone with an old-fashioned horn on a table; in the play it is in a pile of furniture at rear.[5]

Once we take the painting as a text with various meanings within a surreal ground, Stoppard's play may represent that it is not self-existent because of its intertextuality. The text, from the very beginning, leads one to be lost in ambiguity, and uncertainty. In the opening scene, the fruit basket hangs down from the ceiling as a counterbalance of the lamp. This is because the counterbalance with slugs from a .22 calibre pistol was damaged. The furniture is like a barricade because Thelma and Harris are going to go over their final dance. Harris wears a wader because the tub in the bathroom was full of water, as he was trying to replace a bulb there. However, the imagery in the room is like a Magritte painting that signifies crime for Inspector Foot. Therefore, "our sense of knowing the reality has been shaken, the world appears to be stranger than we might have expected."[6] As in a surreal image, a fixed meaning may not be perceived. Even the opening scene is like a surreal view, as Holmes spies on the Harrises. As for the detective story and solve-the-mystery situation, Sophocles' *Oedipus* is a pioneer that aims to solve a murder mystery. However, through the character Foot, *After Magritte* parodies the search of truth. The name Oedipus means "swollen foot," and as is the case in that play, Inspector Foot searches for the truth. However, a quest begins when he puts both his feet in one leg of his pyjama trousers. As Oedipus does not doubt himself, neither does Foot who is indeed in search of a non-existing robbery, and amputation.

After Magritte is a one-act play that may be classified as a comedy and a parody of detective story. Although each character declares that s/he knows the truth as regards what they supposed to be true, the text throws suspicion on the confidence of reason that the Western Philosophy has put on since Plato, and Aristotle. For example, the investigation by Police Constable Holmes, and Detective Inspector Foot turns into such a failure that the text leads one to think the credibility of detective fiction in which the mystery of a crime is solved by investigation and the logical implications of a detective. Therefore, the text challenges the reliability of detective stories through the portrayal of such two police officers. Inspector Foot's calculations and his observations do not bring a hypothesis that leads to order, as otherwise expected within a detective story.

---

5 Natalie Crohn Schmitt, "Window/Picture: L'assassin menacé and Artist Descending a Staircase," *Twentieth Century Literature* 45, no. 3 (1999): 398.

6 Anna Suwalska-Kolecka, "Tom Stoppard's After Magritte: The World of Uncertainty," *Acta Neophilologica* 3 (2001): 297.

Apart from Foot's hypothesis, the police surveillance by Holmes is also parodied by manners, and dialogues; therefore, this is not an Althuserrian surveillance that terrorizes or alarms the Harrises. As Holmes gazes at the scene in Harrises' room in which "most of the furniture is stacked up against the street door in a sort of barricade," Mother is lying on an ironing board.[7] However, Thelma calls an ambulance, as the mother's foot is burned because of the iron. Yet, as she draws the curtains, Holmes says, "It's the police!" to which Thelma replies, "I asked for an ambulance!."[8] Meanwhile, Inspector Foot introduces himself: "I am Chief Inspector Foot" to which Harris says, "Not Foot of the Y-" as he "rises to his feet with a broad enchanted smile."[9] Using language, Harris tries to mock the inspector; yet Foot realizes that mockery by the first letter of Yard which is a measure that equals to three feet. The limb foot is a smaller unit of a yard as is the case in the hierarchy and ranks of the Scotland Yard. Yet, the text may not reveal what Harris supposes by his utterance of "Y-" as he is silenced by Inspector Foot. Therefore, neither speech nor writing is enough to reveal what is meant there. The meaning and the hierarchy between these binary oppositions is lost forever.

The dialogues represent that any signifier may not have a corresponding signified. As the meaning of a signifier depends also on what it does not mean, and what it is not, its meaning may not be fixated. For example, the man that Harris, Thelma, and Mother saw on their way back home is described in different ways by each. As regards the different ways of depictions, Jadwiga Uchman has put it,

> they make use of their individual, subjective impressions and employ language as a means of describing them. Stoppard seems to prove that language can sometimes cause big misunderstandings. While reality is open to different interpretations (especially if it is such a strange, bizarre reality of the hopping figure), the language itself, too, is very often ambiguous and imprecise. Therefore [,] a sentence may sometimes also be open to a number of different interpretations.[10]

In linguistic terms, they cannot settle over a fixed description of the man they saw earlier. For Thelma, he is a "one-legged footballer" with a "football" and a "never-say-die spirit," whereas, for Harris, that man "was carrying a tortoise" and "he was wearing pyjamas."[11] Each time, Harris or Thelma tries to construct

---

7 Stoppard, *Plays 1*, 49.

8 Ibid., 53.

9 Ibid., 59.

10 Jadwiga Uchman, "Words and Images: Tom Stoppard's After Magritte," *Acta Universitatis Lodziensis Litteraria Anglica* 3 (1999): 134.

11 Stoppard, *Plays 1*, 51–52.

a meaning through the description of man, man, as the signifier, seems to be lost in an open-ended existence and non-existence, as each signifies the signifier through "misapprehension."[12] Thelma and Harris describe the man in such contradictory ways that mystery and conflict rule over both speech and the text. This is not the only issue that they cannot come to an agreement. They are not sure whose "mother" it is in their house:

Harris: ... When I married you I didn't expect to have your mother –
Thelma: (Shouting back at him) She's not my mother – she's *your* mother!
Harris: Rubbish ... My mother is a ... tall ... aristocratic woman, in a red mac ... answers to the name of ...[13]

As regards the man-woman opposition, neither Thelma nor Harris is represented to be superior to the other. Both try to fix something in the house, and both are getting ready for a dance. The way they speak is similar to one another. However, various meanings and interpretations exist; therefore, there is no unchangeable one truth for any character. As Derrida remarks, "[t]he presence of an element is always a signifying and substitutive reference inscribed in a system of differences and the movement of a chain."[14] The utterances of the characters on whose mother it is bring forth a play of presence and absence. The characters are not clear in mind and they are confused. Therefore, the text deals with "the confusion brought about by an improper understanding of an iconic or linguistic sign."[15]

For Foot, the room, and the behaviour of the three, is a "bizarre spectacle."[16] He may not arrive at a reasonable meaning because of what he sees, and he says, "This is a disorderly house."[17] Although Harris remarks that "[t]here is obviously a perfectly logical reason for everything," Foot states that "[t]he disorderliness I was referring to consists of immoral conduct."[18] By the time Harris asks for "a search warrant," Foot sticks up for Holmes as "[h]e's not one of your TV heroes," for Foot, Holmes "is doing his job ... well."[19] Holmes is like an opposite of Arthur

---

12 Ibid., 54.
13 Ibid., 57.
14 Jacques Derrida, Writing and Difference, trans. Alan Bass (London: Routledge, 2002), 369.
15 Uchman, "Words and Images," 140.
16 Stoppard, *Plays 1*, 58.
17 Ibid., 63.
18 Ibid., 63.
19 Ibid., 60–61.

Conan Doyle's Sherlock Holmes. He does not even know what a "search warrant" is: "To tell you the truth, sir, I'm not absolutely sure what a search warrant looks like."[20] Yet, Foot hides his displeasure, and asks about the ".22 calibre pistols." They were in "the broken halves of the porcelain container that had held the slugs and acted as the counterweight to the light fitting."[21] Whether the investigation progresses or not is not clear, as no one may signify the intended meaning in the other's mind. Each signifier brings another signification, and a transformation of signifiers generates a shift of absence and presence. Therefore, the deference of meaning may not fix any truth:

FOOT: It is my duty to tell you that I am not satisfied with your reply.
THELMA: What was the question?
FOOT: That is hardly the point.

Questions and replies contradict to an extent that Foot's investigation becomes a "game of cat and mouse" as Harris calls it. Questions follow one another:

FOOT: (snaps) Do you often stack the furniture up against the door?
THELMA: Yes, is that a crime?
FOOT: (furiously) Will you stop trying to exploit my professional knowledge for your private ends! – I didn't do twenty years of hard grind to have my brains picked by every ignorant layman who finds out I'm a copper![22]

Although Foot tries to seem confident, Thelma, Harris, and the mother do not take him seriously. Foot charges them with "amputation": "I have reason to believe that within the last hour in this room you performed without anaesthetic an illegal operation on a bold nigger minstrel about five-foot-two or Pakistani and that is only the beginning!."[23] Inspector Foot takes the absurd situation of the room for such an accusation, as he trusts in Holmes, and his "professional knowledge."[24] As may be the case in René Magritte's surrealist paintings, ways of seeing differ in the text, as meaning is almost always deferred.

Although Foot aims to be accepted as a practical, tough-minded detective, his intention may not be grasped by the others. As is the case in Sartre's existentialist play *No Exit* (1944), none of the characters in *After Magritte* may attain their intended being. Regarding being and existence, Sartre remarks that "man first of

20 Ibid., 61.
21 Ibid., 61–62
22 Ibid., 62.
23 Ibid., 62.
24 Ibid., 62.

all exists, encounters himself, surges up in the world – and defines himself afterwards."[25] For Sartre, "existence precedes essence"; therefore, one exists, and after that, s/he tries to establish her/his self. Sartre clarifies his statement:

> That being is man, or, as Heidegger put it, the human reality. What do we mean here by "existence precedes essence"? We mean that man first exists: he materializes in the world, encounters himself, and only afterward defines himself. If man as existentialists conceive of him cannot be defined, it is because to begin with he is nothing. He will not be anything until later, and then he will he what he makes of himself.[26]

Neither the case in interrogation nor the characters and their speeches may be defined within the text. Not only the characters but also the text defers its meaning. Therefore, a clash of existence and absence lurks in the meaningless dialogues. For Sartre, there exist two kinds of beings: that are conscious, "being for itself," and that are not conscious, "being in itself." As Sartre has put it, "man shall attain existence only when he is what he projects himself to be – not what he would like to be."[27] Foot "would like to be" and act as if he were a professional detective superior to his police Holmes. Yet, he may not assure his existence as a trustable detective because even Holmes is unconscious of Foot's actions and intentions. No one is conscious of another's projections; therefore, alongside meaning, existence is also deferred. Although each character is responsible of what s/he says and how s/he acts, none seems to attain an essence. For example, Harris tries to fix house utilities, but his actions seem to be odd to Foot and Holmes; because of his actions they even suppose that he is after an amputation. Foot believes that he is a practical detective but even Holmes is not aware of Foot's suppositions.

For Sartre, actions through free choice may create meaning. Yet, the mother, for example, does not act to play the tuba. She keeps asking to play it: "Can I practice now?,"[28] "Is it all right for me to practice?,"[29] "I only practice on the tuba"[30] and "Can I have a go now?".[31] Neither Foot nor Thelma or Harris answers her, and she does not play it. The same is true for Harris who may not fix the bulb or the counterweight, and true for Foot. Therefore, their intended actions

25 Jean Paul Sartre, Existentialism Is a Humanism, trans. Carol Macomber (London: Yale University Press, 2007), 22.

26 Ibid., 22.

27 Stoppard, *Plays 1*, 23.

28 Ibid., 59.

29 Ibid., 60.

30 Ibid., 63.

31 Ibid., 65.

are not materialized. Thus, meaning is not fixed from an existentialist view. If we take their actions, inactions, and intentions as signifiers, none of the signifiers have a pre-fixed, and present meaning. When Foot asks about the amputation, the mother asks about playing the tuba:

FOOT: The D.P.P. is going to take a very poor view if you have been offering cut-price amputations to immigrant … What we're looking for is a darkie short of a leg or two.
HOLMES: (retiring) Right, sir.
MOTHER: Is it all right for me to practice?[32]

For both the mother and Foot, no meaning exists as regards what the other says. Irrationality and lack of clarity are perceived to be the meaning of such meaningless dialogues. The sign system within the text collapses in such a deep absence that the existence of meaning is lost beyond the text. As referentiality of utterances ceases to exist, contradictions dominate on the text to such an extent that meaning is continuously deferred. The meaning stumbles itself within the text. Although the characters act and speak through their intended objects, the other(s) may not comprehend it. Meanings of thoughts and words remain in-between the essence and the existence as the intentional essence may not establish a connection with neither the system of language nor the world around.

As Foot goes on interrogation, Harris, Mother, and Thelma's explanations seem irrational and meaningless to Foot. As he speaks, Harris is confused about whose mother the "mother" is: "my wife's mother, in law, or rather my mother, prevailed upon us to take her to the exhibition."[33] However, their explanation gets absurd and meaningless for each:

HARRIS: We went to see an exhibition of surrealistic art at the Tate Gallery.
FOOT: I must say that in a lifetime of off-the-cuff alibis I have seldom been moved closer to open derision.
THELMA: Perhaps it would help to explain that my-mother-in-law is a devotee of Maigret.
MOTHER: Magritte.[34]

Although Thelma's confusion of the name may arouse humour, the name "Maigret" is a fictional character created by the Belgian writer Georges Joseph Simenon (1903–1989). Therefore, the relationship of the text to other texts, its intertextuality, represses the idea that the text is a closed one. The text contains

32 Ibid., 63.
33 Ibid., 65.
34 Ibid., 66.

the traces of others: Maigret, the detective Sherlock Holmes, and René Magritte's painting. Intertextuality is inherent within the text through Sherlock Holmes-like detective story, Magritte-like scenery, structure, and form of the text. Such pre-existing texts are transformed and parodied within *After Magritte*. The mother tries to comment on René Magritte's paintings on tuba: "Tubas on fire, tubas stuck to lions and naked women, tubas hanging in the sky – there was one woman with a tuba with a sack over her head as far as I could make out. I doubt he'd ever tried to play one; in fact if you ask me the man must have been some kind of lunatic."[35] The explanation is meaningless because the mother who is a devotee of Magritte seems to be confused about the meanings of his paintings. After all, the exhibition, for her, "was a disappointment."[36]

Holmes, Foot, and the others feel alien to one another, as meaning may not be established. What one thinks may not be comprehended by the other(s). From a post-structuralist approach, the binary opposition of thought/language is at work here. "Thought" may not exist prior to "language." The rules of the society shape the language through which an individual thinks and speaks. Thought, language, and utterances within the text do not comply with the concept of logocentrism. The parodied character Holmes does not signify a police officer who is aware of what goes around. The signifier-signified relationship is not of service within the text, and the speeches of the characters are not appreciated within the text. The descriptions of the man that Thelma, Harris, and Mother saw on their way back home are different from one another; therefore, the speech does not bring forth the truth. However, Foot's accusations do not disclose any truth. The mother's love of Magritte does not represent her true ideas on him since she regards the painter as "lunatic." The insufficiency of language is represented through the text; that is, the text "displays[s] the insufficiency of language when it strives for an origin beyond all reach."[37] The utterances of the characters remind the supposition that "man finds in things nothing but what he himself has imported into them."[38] The desires of the characters shape and reshape meaning independent of each other, as "meaning is a construct brought by the "subject," a fiction made by the force of our desire."[39] Language, ambiguous and slippery within the text,

35 Ibid., 66.

36 Ibid., 66.

37 Christopher Norris, Deconstruction: Theory and Practice (London: Routledge, 1991), 36.

38 G. Douglas Atkins, Reading Deconstruction/Deconstructive Reading (Kentucky: The University Press of Kentucky, 1983), 29.

39 Ibid., 29.

does not lead the characters to communicate as they desire.[40] The signifiers may not comprehend the intended signified:

HARRIS: … he may have been a sort of street arab making off with his lute …
THELMA: His *loot*?
HARRIS: … or his mandolin-…[41]

Although Saussure has put it, "[t]he linguistic sign unites, not a thing and a name, but a concept and a sound-image," Thelma gets another signified. The dissemination of the signifier is at such an extent that other meanings are established although the other(s) may not grasp that point.[42] That leads the signifier "loot" and/or "lute" to defer meaning. The sound image and the concept are different for Thelma and Harris; therefore, what exists in one's mind is absent in the other's. The "trace" of other instruments is mingled; Thelma and Harris may not comprehend the differences of the signifiers. As Madan Sarup remarks, "in each sign there are traces of the other words which that sign has excluded in order to be itself."[43] Signifiers postpone meaning; therefore, language may not establish a proper communication. The text becomes a play of "différance."

Their interpretations of whoever they saw becomes fictious just like the clash of signifier and signified that does not comply with one another. New and different ways of thinking emerge. The text separates and breaks off the relationship between the signifier and the signified several times. The process of communication among the characters becomes circular. Meaning is not present in the signifier. Foot relies on an eye-witness' account; yet it seems to be a fictious one although Foot takes it to be true. Individual perceptions and interpretations do not bring a fixed meaning. Each utterance of a character constitutes a plurality of perceptions because one perceives a sign of the thing, not the thing itself. All characters have different ideologies, lifestyles, and backgrounds that shape their use of language. Each other's language creates a kind of meaning that is foreign to the other(s).

Logocentric and phonocentric beliefs of the Western philosophy make speech superior over writing and such a belief system looks for a transcendental signified. However, language comprises signifiers that are incorporated into one

---

40 Lois Tyson, Critical Theory Today: A User-Friendly Guide (London: Routledge, 2006), 250.

41 Stoppard, *Plays 1*, 56.

42 Ibid., 67.

43 Madan Sarup, An Introductory Guide to Post-Structuralism and Postmodernism (New York: Harvester, 1993), 36.

another to an extent that no transcendental signifier may cease such an endless deferment of meaning.[44] Although speech is believed to represent the unity of the speaker's ideas, communication stumbles several times within the text. This condition may lead meaning to defer within the context that reconstructs various meanings.[45] Each time understanding is supposed to be generated, another deferment calls out another reality. Deferment may lead human actions to have possible meanings, as there is no unique reference between the signifier and the signified.[46] However, at such times speech and writing may fail to give meaning.

Truth and fiction are mingled to such a point that what exists and what does not are reversed. Thus far, any mental "trace" of a signifier is composed of differences. As regards the reversal of hierarchies, Atkins has put it,

> "believing is seeing" and interpretation is all there is. Clearly, however, Derrida is not nihilistic … for he insists throughout that consciousness is no origin, no foundation, there being no foundation. He undoes the truth/fiction, reality/ consciousness polarities but not, with the advocates of the autonomous consciousness, so as to set up the second term in the place of the first. Fiction can no more exist without truth than truth without fiction or presence without absence; they are accomplices, the system of differences and the "trace" making truth (im)possible. By the same token, the subject "in itself," as center, origin, and goal, is no more possible than the object "in itself."[47]

Meaning changes throughout the play as the signifier and signified do not have stable manners in the minds of the characters. As meaning is not stable, what exists and what does not produce a never-ending deferral, and meaning is postponed. Sartre's idea on the relationship between existence and essence may be reread by Camus' ideas on the idea of death and estrangement. As regards the ideas of both thinkers, one may or may not create his desired self through his aims. Regarding existence, Sartre has put it, "[m]an is not only that which he conceives himself to be, but that which he wills himself to be, and since he conceives of himself only after lie exists, just as he wills himself to be after being thrown into existence, man is nothing other than what he makes of himself. This is the first principle of existentialism."[48] Foot regards himself to be a practical

---

44 Zeynep Direk, *Çağdaş Kıta Felsefesi-Bergson'dan Derrida'ya-* (İstanbul: Fol Kitap, 2021), 280.

45 Aslı Özlem Tarakcıoğlu, "Anlamın Sonsuzluğu Üzerine: Post-Yapısalcılık ve Yapısöküm Perspektifinden 'Mutlu Sonlar'," In *Edebiyat Kuramları: Giriş ve Uygulama*, edited by Mehmet Akif Balkaya and Kuğu Tekin (Konya: Çizgi, 2019), 64.

46 Berna Moran, *Edebiyat Kuramları ve Eleştiri*, (İstanbul: İletişim Yayınları, 2009), 202.

47 Atkins, Reading Deconstruction, 29.

48 Sartre, Existentialism Is a Humanism, 22.

detective; yet, he seems to be irrational through his accusations which in time are regarded to be absurd. As Camus "limit[s] [him]self to existential philosophies," he supposes that the "inability to understand becomes the existence."[49] Within the play, signifiers may not correspond to an intended signified as signified is also deferred. Therefore, a reasonable meaning may not be attained since irrational utterances (for each character) challenge reasons. As regards the relation between existence and irrationality, Camus remarks that "[t]he theme of the irrational, as it is conceived by the existentialists, is reason becoming confused and escaping by negating itself."[50]

The idea of existence and absence and the concept of meaninglessness bring forth Albert Camus' ideas on the absurd. The ideas of death and estrangement are two major features of absurd existence. As Camus has put it, "man feels an alien, a stranger. … the feeling of absurdity" is a result of "this divorce between man and his life."[51] For Camus, a man that thinks of his own suicide has "a direct connection between this feeling and the longing for death." Camus, in *The Myth of Sisyphus*, remarks that man accepts and recognizes the absurd; therefore, it stopped to be the absurd. This recognition and acceptance give hope to escape from that condition. Clarity of meaning is lost because of the irrational deductions through dialogues as any signified is signified and decoded in irrational ways by the other characters. Although the relationship between the signifier and the signified is "a convention accepted by all users of a given language"[52] the signified of one character' utterance may become another signifier for the other; therefore, the signified may signify something else for the other. Thus, the characters seem to lose a meaningful dialogue. As regards clarity and such an irrationality, Camus has put it, "[A]t this point of his effort man stands face to face with the irrational. He feels within him his longing for happiness and for rationality. The absurd is born of this confrontation between the human need and the unreasonable silence of the world."[53] The mother and Foot are now aware of what really goes around. They are after "happiness" and "rationality" on their interpretations. The mother's "need" is to play the tuba, and Foot's "need" is to be accepted as a respectable detective; yet the meaningless dialogues among the characters bring forth such a chaos that the text seems to be lost in it. Each

49 Albert Camus, The Myth of Sisyphus, trans. Justin O'brien (London: Penguin, 1979), 35–36.

50 Ibid., 49.

51 Ibid., 13.

52 David Lodge, Modern Criticism and Theory (London: Pearson, 2000), 1.

53 Camus, The Myth of Sisyphus, 32.

character is represented to be alienated as in Camus' *The Myth of Sisyphus*. However, like Magritte's paintings, anyone may have his/her way of interpretation by examining the text. Since the characters may not attain their desired objects, "[a] total absence of hope" takes place.[54] Therefore, the text seems to be open-ended as for the events and the characters, and in Camus' words, "It is that divorce between the mind that desires and the world that disappoints."[55] Foot's and the mother's desires may not be satisfied within the text.

Although Foot aims to act like an authoritative figure, his suppositions are not objectively interpreted. Toward the end of the play, the misunderstandings get explanations. In a haste to park his car to the only park meter that Harrrises left, Foot put both of his feet on the same leg of his pyjamas, and he had his wife's bag as it had some change and parasol. That may be the man that attracted the Harrises, yet they are not objective with their descriptions. Therefore, meaning is deferred several times within the clash of subjectivity and objectivity. Each of their knowledge is influenced, and objectivity becomes subjectivity in disguise. Foot, the mother, Harris and Thelma's use of language seems to be shaped differently through their experience and knowledge. The human conscious does not generate the same language and meaning for all. Therefore, the meaning of existence may not be figured out. All the supposedly existing deductions collapse one by one. The language produces evolving, dynamic and "ideologically saturated operations."[56] Each utterance disseminates infinite number of meanings. Therefore, "there is no center to our understanding of existence."[57] The text has no final meaning, and it remains a place of possibilities.[58]

Foot remarks, "After Magritte you apparently returned to your car parked in Ponsonby Place, and drove off at the very moment and from the very spot where the escaping minstrel was last observed, which suggest to me that you may have kept a rendezvous and driven off with him in your car."[59] He asks for a witness, and then they talk about the man in various interpretations. For example, Thelma and Harris comprehended "lute" in different ways:

HARRIS: Since the fellow was blind he needn't necessarily have known it was a tortoise. He might have picked it up in mistake for some other object such as a lute.

---

54 Ibid., 34.
55 Ibid., 50.
56 Tyson, Critical Theory Today, 256.
57 Ibid., 256.
58 Hans Bertens, Literary Theory: The Basics (London: Routledge, 2001), 131.
59 Stoppard, *Plays 1*, 67.

FOOT:	His loot?
HARRIS:	Or mandolin.
MOTHER:	It was, in fact, an alligator handbag.
FOOT:	I'm afraid I can't accept these picturesque fantasies. My wife has an alligator handbag and I defy anyone to mistake it for a musical instrument.
THELMA:	STOP! Don't move! (They desist.) I've dropped the needle.[60]

Foot perceives the signifier "lute" with another signifier; the musical instrument becomes stolen things in Foot's mind. If "[l]anguage can also be compared with a sheet of paper: thought is the front and the sound the back,"[61] then why does Foot think of the stolen money instead of a musical instrument. The sheet of paper seems to work in different ways for different receivers; therefore, as soon as a meaning exists for one, it immediately becomes absent for the other. "[T]he absence of certain words partly creates and certainly winnows and refines the meanings of those that are present."[62] Part of the meaning of "lute" was supposed to be created by its difference from "loot." However, each character takes what is absent as what is present, and the chaos deepens. Foot desires to act in an authoritative way, yet the others do not pay attention to his intended meaning. Foot supposes that he stands for rationality. However, the authority representative in a detective fiction turns into a comic figure who is not aware of his ridiculous side. Although Foot is signified as the authority, Thelma dictates them to "STOP! Don't move!."[63] The image of power is embedded in Thelma in a funny way. Foot's firm sense of identity as the representative of authority is shaken several times. All Foot's "hypothesis" about the supposedly crimes of the Harrises are not related to fact. Inspector Foot is no superior to Holmes or "Sherlock Holmes." Foot does not have the "respectable detective" identity that exists in his imagination. Foot's demand on objective truth and his reliability is deconstructed by the text itself.

Just like the mother who is represented as a tuba player – yet who does not play it – Foot's desire to act like a respected detective is deferred recurrently. However, Foot does not reply when the mother asks whether she may play her tuba; therefore, that act is also deferred. As Hans Bertens states, "language is inherently unreliable" and it "operates on the basis of differentiation."[64] A dynamic state

60 Ibid., 68.

61 Ferdinand de Saussure, Course in General Linguistics, trans. Wade Baskin (New York: Philosophical Library, 1959), 114.

62 Terence Hawkes, Structuralism and Semiotics (London: Routledge, 2003), 15.

63 Stoppard, *Plays 1*, 67.

64 Bertens, Literary Theory, 124.

of change prevails the text, as it is self-destructed through the deferment of meaning.

The text lacks the accuracy on the issue whether the conception and the way the characters think precede their experiences. The signifiers construct a chain that is always at work which enables infinite meanings to be deduced. Language is used in such a way that almost no stability, and/or no final meaning may be established. As Tyson has put it, "The ambiguous, ideological nature of language explain[s] many of the difficulties" the characters within the text "... encounter in communicating with others."[65] Therefore, language used in the text is so dynamic and unfixed that possible meanings are constructed. As in a postmodern fiction, the characters and their perceptions are so different from one another that the reader may not decide which is true in the final case. Yet, the characters seem not to be disturbed by such various meanings; on the contrary, they are indifferent to this point. This is an issue that challenges the opposition of absence and existence. Any reader may choose his/her way to read the text because "[m]eaning is created by the reader in the act of reading."[66] Although, in the end of the play, the mystery seems to be solved, the final may be realized as ambiguous by anyone who witnesses the end, just like the beginning of the play:

(1) MOTHER, standing on her good foot only, on the wooden chair, which is placed on the table; a woollen sock on one hand, playing the tuba.
(2) Lightshade, slowly descending toward the table.
(3) FOOT, with one bare foot, sunglasses, eating banana.
(4) Fruit basket, slowly ascending.
(5) HARRIS, gowned, blindfolded with a cushion over his head, arms outstretched, on one leg, counting.

THELMA, in underwear, crawling around the table, scanning the floor and niffing. HOLMES reoils into paralysis.

FOOT: Well, Constable, I think you owe us all an explanation.[67]

Harris is blindfolded, and on one leg because he tries to comprehend whether "a blind man can ... stand on one leg!" as Foot has just suggested. Yet, like Foot's "best man, Sergeant Potter,"[68] any newcomer to this scenery would have several meanings. The text implies that the scenery may remain in between existence

65 Tyson, Critical Theory Today, 258.

66 Ibid., 258.

67 Stoppard, *Plays 1*, 72.

68 Ibid., 65.

and absence as the final of the text suggests: "The lampshade descends inexorably as the music continues to play; when it touches the table-top, there is no more light. Alternatively, the lampshade could disappear down the horn of the tuba."[69] No final meaning is established, as the play almost ends in where it begins by "producing a circular effect to the action – which could, it seems, start all over again."[70] Regarding this circularity, Brian Crossley remarks, "[t]his circularity of design therefore denies in After Magritte the sense of an ending."[71] However, the light and darkness opposition, from the beginning to the end, is repeated as Foot wears a sock on his hand and holds the hot light bulb while he eats banana, and wears sunglasses to get rid of his migraine. Everything on the scene and/or the text may "disappear down the horn of the tuba," as the supposedly dark sides of interrogation may not come into light.

To conclude, any interpretation may not materialize a final meaning. Therefore, the text "consist[s] of a multiplicity of overlapping, conflicting meanings in dynamic, fluid relation to one another."[72] What the text may reveal is undecidable. The meaning within the text is conflicting and plural from different perceptions of the reader and the characters. Through the images, perceptions of the characters and events within the text, any meaning, and what exists through that meaning, defers itself to an unknown period; therefore, possible meanings may be established. The end of the play may bring forth more interpretations which may go on producing possible other meanings. What exists for one may be absent for the other(s) as meaning is deferred all time alongside the text. Stoppard's play undermines wholeness within the meaning of the text itself.

An open-ended text paves way to infinite meanings. The characters seem to be lost in the absence of existence, as they are self-assured to find meaning in the middle of a meaningless condition. Differences of meanings – which the characters believe to establish – differ, substitute and complete each other. The text presents that what is supposed to be existing is not present. The hierarchical such binary oppositions as presence/absence, meaningful/meaningless, speech/writing and reason/passion are jumbled up into a chaos, and disordered state, as meaning is postponed each time within the play. The changing perceptions of the characters may represent that meaning may not be fixed, and it is not

---

69 Ibid., 72.

70 Christopher Hahn, "The Theatre of Tom Stoppard: The Spectator as Hero." MA Thesis, 1979: 31.

71 Brian M. Crossley, "An Investigation of Stoppard's 'Hound' and 'Foot,'" *Modern Drama* 20, no. 1 (1977): 84. Project *MUSE*.

72 Tyson, Critical Theory Today, 259.

self-existent within the text because no centralized meaning is present within the text. Therefore, as Derrida has put it, "language bears within itself the necessity of its own critique."[73] The characters through their utterances, words, and perceptions may not achieve presence, as their speeches may not represent reality. The wholeness of the text may not be achieved, as no objectivity lurks because of the repercussions of a surreal image as represented through the Harrises' room and perceptions. However, the absence of a sign both determines and undermines the presence of a signified within the text. Thus, a shift of presence and absence prevails the text, as the signifiers and the signifieds may be combined continually. The text has plenty of signifiers that contradict one another in such a way that meaning is continuously deferred.

Bibliography

Atkins, G. Douglas. *Reading Deconstruction/Deconstructive Reading*. Kentucky: The University Press of Kentucky, 1983.

Bennett, Jonathan. "Philosophy and Mr. Stoppard." *Philosophy* 50, no. 191 (1975): 5–18. https://www.jstor.org/stable/3749568

Bertens, Hans. *Literary Theory: The Basics*. London: Routledge, 2001.

Camus, Albert. *The Myth of Sisyphus*. Trans. Justin O'brien. Penguin: London, 1979.

Crossley, Brian M. "An Investigation of Stoppard's 'Hound' and 'Foot'." *Modern Drama* 20, no. 1 (1977): 77–86. https://muse.jhu.edu/article/497496/pdf

Derrida, Jacques. *Writing and Difference*. Trans. Alan Bass. London: Routledge, 2002.

Direk, Zeynep. *Çağdaş Kıta Felsefesi-Bergson'dan Derrida'ya-*. Fol Kitap, 2021.

Hahn, Christopher. *The Theatre of Tom Stoppard: The Spectator as Hero*. MA Thesis, The University of Cape Town, 1979.

Hawkes, Terence. *Structuralism and Semiotics*. London: Routledge, 2003.

Kelly, Katherine E. "Tom Stoppard's "Artist Descending A Staircase": Outdoing the 'Dada' Duchamp." *Comparative Drama* 20, no. 3 (1986): 191–200. https://www.jstor.org/stable/41153243

Lodge, David. *Modern Criticism and Theory*. London: Pearson, 2000.

Moran, Berna. *Edebiyat Kuramları ve Eleştiri*. İstanbul: İletişim Yayınları, 2009.

Norris, Christopher. *Deconstruction: Theory and Practice*. London: Routledge, 1991.

Sartre, Jean Paul. *Existentialism Is a Humanism*. Trans. Carol Macomber. London: Yale University Press, 2007.

73 Derrida, Writing and Difference, 358.

Sarup, Madan. *An Introductory Guide to Post-Structuralism and Postmodernism*. New York: Harvester, 1993.

Saussure, Ferdinand de. *Course in General Linguistics*. Trans. Wade Baskin. New York: Philosophical Library, 1959.

Schmitt, Natalie Crohn. "Window/Picture: L'assassin menacé and Artist Descending a Staircase." *Twentieth Century Literature* 45, no. 3 (1999): 385–400. https://www.jstor.org/stable/441926

Stoppard, Tom. *Tom Stoppard: Plays 1*. London: Faber & Faber, 1996.

Suwalska-Kolecka, Anna. "Tom Stoppard's After Magritte: The World of Uncertainty." *Acta Neophilologica* 3 (2001): 289–299. http://cejsh.icm.edu.pl›cejsh›element›289-299.

Tarakcıoğlu, Aslı Özlem. "Anlamın Sonsuzluğu Üzerine: Post-Yapısalcılık ve Yapısöküm Perspektifinden 'Mutlu Sonlar'." In *Edebiyat Kuramları: Giriş ve Uygulama*, edited by Mehmet Akif Balkaya and Kuğu Tekin. Konya: Çizgi, 2019: 59–85.

Tyson, Lois. *Critical Theory Today: A User-Friendly Guide*. London: Routledge, 2006.

Uchman, Jadwiga. "Words and Images: Tom Stoppard's After Magritte." *Acta Universitatis Lodziensis Litteraria Anglica* 3 (1999): 129–141. http://cejsh.icm.edu.pl/cejsh/element/bwmeta1.element.hdl_11089_14419?q=bwmeta1.element.hdl_11089_12871-1999-3;1&qt=CHILDREN-STATELESS

Gül Kurtuluş

Memory, Gender and Innovation in Caryl Churchill's *Cloud Nine*: The Brechtian Legacy in the Postmodern Theatre

Introduction

During the 1970s and 1980s the term "theatre" was deficient in describing modernist work and the term "performance art" became more popular and encompassing. Theatre has always been closely attached to a certain tradition, which requires a conventionally composed script, a specific type of narrative structure, and a presentation or performance in an accustomed manner. A rise in the new interest of the avant-garde seen in spectacle activities of various kinds prepared the ground for the presentation of new non-structured events. A blend of dance and theatre has been exhibited via the media, especially with the utilization of film and video. Such innovations and experiments have been coined as postmodern theatre, "characterized through its emphasis on voice and image, rather than on narrative and character, emphasizing the collective and interactive over the individual and self-sufficient text."[1] Current changes give a new shape and content to theatrical activities in England. Like female dramatists who actively produced works during the last decades of the twentieth century, Caryl Churchill has presented political concerns in her plays. Social and political concerns combined with innovative staging and style typify the work of Caryl Churchill. With her unique language and style, Churchill goes beyond her time and expands traditional feminist views and theories. It is possible to confer her language and narrative in tandem with characteristics of postmodern drama and examine her work in view of postmodern feminist theory taking into consideration *Cloud Nine* (1979) that bears postmodern elements.

Cloud Nine exposes the issues of sex/gender constructions and sexuality within a patriarchal and heteronormative framework that is also very much sexist and racist, and challenges established norms and expectations related to sexuality and gender. Churchill achieves this firstly by cross-acting; she makes men play female characters, and women play male characters, and a White actor plays a

---

1 Jeanette R. Malkin, Memory-Theatre and Postmodern Drama (Ann Arbor: The University of Michigan Press, 1999), 17.

Black character (there is also a dummy instead of an actress in the first act). Using Brechtian methods, she reverses the social positions of characters and puts them in absurd situations, thereby exposing and criticizing patriarchy. She also utilizes manipulation of time to establish gender as a social construct. Patriarchal and colonialist values are depicted evanescing. Characters and conditions immensely change in hundred years, and Churchill proffers that times indeed change, and nothing ever stays permanent. Despite the oppression by those in powers in the second act, a lot of power has shifted from the male authority to women and homosexuals. All characters, including Betty, have the freedom to explore and talk about their sexuality in the second act. Caryl Churchill does not have a lot of care for people's sensibilities, but the shocking effect serves to emphasize the absurdity of the power balance between genders that men seem to simply dominate in the first act. To Churchill, sexuality is a powerful element in feminist discourse; especially female sexuality and homosexuality are toxic for patriarchy, and this is perhaps why the play is so full of sex. This chapter aims to explore Caryl Churchill's *Cloud Nine* in relation to history, memory and audience's role in making the play an intersection between Brechtian and post-Brechtian theatre, and also postmodernist theatre. Furthermore, the chapter intends to offer a reading of the play in tandem with postmodernism in theatre.

British Political Playwriting and Memory

Caryl Churchill and other British political playwrights focus on a deeper and more general discussion of political issues, and in their plays, they prefer more conventional types of theatrical styles which are reflectionist and interventionist.[2] The reflectionist tradition promotes reality and it aims to imitate nature as accurately as possible, which makes it the representation of life itself. A dramatic framework is used to narrate the events in the play. Its plot structure is conventional (exposition, development, and denouement). Characters in the plays are representatives of their social types, and dialogues communicate the ideas stated in the play. Political insights stated in the play depend on a consensus. Milena Dragićević Šešić and Milena Stefanović suggest that "collective memories leading towards 'national memory' help construct national identity and representation."[3] Accordingly, reflectionist tradition in theatre contributes to the

2 Michael Patterson, Strategies of Political Theatre: Post-War British Playwrights (Cambridge: Cambridge University Press, 2003), 15.

3 Milena Dragićević Šešić and Milena Stefanović, "How Theaters Remember: Cultures of Memory in Institutionalized Systems," *Култура/Culture* 24, no. 4 (2014): 11–12.

national memory because it aims to convey political message(s) to the audience. In reflectionist plays, the audience is expected to measure the political analysis in a realistic plot and compare themselves to the theatrical characters in the play.

Different than the reflectionist tradition, the interventionist tradition promotes the interpretation of reality. It aims to challenge people's perception of reality. Lauren Harlow claims that history and memory are different from one another and that one should not mistake one for the other. "History is the use of collected facts and primary sources in effort to create a living conversation between the past and present [while m]emory on the other hand, how a single person or a group of people chooses to remember these historical facts in relation to their personal lives and cultures."[4] Thus, collective memory is not a fact, but a remembrance. Interventionist playwrights interpret those remembrances of historical facts subjectively because they believe that objectivity controverts their point of view. They object to an established consensual view of the world. "The strategy of this theatre was therefore not to induce empathy with the central characters so much as to judge their behaviour within the social context."[5] Its plot is not traditional because of the lack of a sense of inevitability. The narration of the story is in leaps. The characters in such plays are contradictory and alterable beings. Thus, all of these are different than what the conventional theatre is accustomed to, which leads to an altered audience. In interventionist tradition, audience is more active than in reflectionist tradition. It judges and makes choices throughout the play. As the audience is already knowledgeable about the ending, they focus on the plot development, which encourages them to respond actively.

Reflectionist and interventionist traditions are both used after the 1960s by the political playwrights although they are distinct styles, and interventionist tradition captures the postmodernist world. Bertolt Brecht's interventionist style is efficient in competing with reflectionist tradition as a relatively new mode in dramatic writing. As a Marxist playwright who advocates taking history as a point to consider the present, Brecht makes use of plot structure albeit it is not the focal element of the play. Brecht's epic theatre is the theatre of alienation, and it has the estrangement effect while addressing contemporary issues. It challenges plot structure of well-made plays and leaves issues unresolved, confronting the audience with uncomfortable questions. Political plays originated in Brechtian

4 Lauren Harlow, "The Misconception of Memory: Part One," accessed 15 January 2021, https://stlukesmuseum.org/misconception-memory-hsl-2-2/.

5 Patterson, *Strategies of Political Theatre*, 18.

style make the audience think and evaluate the current situation. Brecht's effort to integrate the audience into his plays actively results in audience's functioning role in theatre. The alienation or estrangement effect enforces the audience to think critically about ethics, morality, power and other socio-economic and political convictions not challenged before and engages them with plays' content actively as well as intellectually rather than emotionally. In her article, Helene Keyssar states, "In Caryl Churchill's plays, neither the sequence nor the unraveling events are central to the drama since she rejects the temptations of narrative and exploits the ability of the live stage to provoke our acknowledgement the vulnerability and plasticity of human."[6] Alienation, disillusionment, immorality, selfishness, and loss of values that Churchill emphasizes in almost all of her plays attract attention as reflections of modern life that the audience is familiar to. Individuals of today move around in a senseless rush, just like Churchill's characters. The modern individual, who speaks the same language with her characters, shares the same concerns, and even lives in the same world, and has become alienated, losing his/her ties with the roots. Doomed to an inevitable loneliness, the individual cannot be happy and able to communicate with those around him. People sometimes resort to violence because they find it difficult to find solutions, and they often live in a fantasy world, escaping reality, as witnessed in Churchill's plays. Since the world they live in is a virtual world, they engage in meaningless and contradictory actions. The degeneration of the individual, and therefore the society, who can no longer distinguish between reality and illusion, gains momentum.

As stated above, Brechtian elements are prominent in *Cloud Nine,* and Churchill's innovative writing styles like gender-bending and comedic tone are significant for expressing the ideas of the play. The historical aspects of the play – colonialism, racial oppression and the traditional gender expectations of the period – provide criticism on social matters with regard to both the time the play is set in and the present time. Reinelt states that "one of Brecht's major discoveries was that by historicizing the incidents of the narrative, a playwright can cause the audience to become conscious of certain habitual perceptions which have been established by the historical tradition and therefore partially determine the present."[7] Churchill uses this technique in *Cloud Nine* as well,

6 Helene Keyssar, "The Dramas of Caryl Churchill: The Politics of Possibility," The Massachusetts Review 24, no. 1 (1983): 198.

7 Janelle Reinelt, "Beyond Brecht: Britain's New Feminist Drama," *Theatre Journal* 38, no. 2 (1986): 160.

effectively creating a bridge between the past and the present. Her comedic tone also plays an important role in portraying the absurdities of extreme gender and identity performance. Especially, on stage, the gender swaps heighten the conventional gender behaviours, standing out when performed by the opposite sex. Diamond explains this as: "When Betty utters the confused clichés of the oppressed Victorian wife, we laugh not only because they are consistent with the stereotypes, we have of that figure but because the stage image is radically disorienting."[8] Thus, Churchill's writing style in *Cloud Nine* shatters the boundaries and invents new ways of expressing political views.

Audience's Role in Political Plays

Borowski suggests that even though different political plays refer to various events in history, the political concern is the same, and this connects all of them.[9] Though the spectators are part of the play on stage, and they have already experienced history, there is an audience with a more extended "collective memory" recently, where plays may find rich contexts and explore from that archive. According to Brecht, non-Aristotelian theatre is the most appropriate method to create awareness about politics.[10] The audience is encouraged to make a choice and criticize so they become part of the political dialogue and actions in the theatre.[11] In alliance with Brechtian terms, epic theatre is the most suitable method to perform a political play. Brechtian techniques comprise breaking down the fourth wall using a narrator, freezing frames, using technology, using minimal settings, coming out of characters. Rather than allowing the audience to sit passively and get lost in the show, the actors will sometimes directly address the audience with a speech, comment or a question. "Brecht's special contribution was to envisage a particular role for the actor in all this, using him to help destroy conventional illusion [and] to arouse a thinking, enquiring response in

8 Elin Diamond, "Refusing the Romanticism of Identity: Narrative Interventions in Churchill, Benmussa, Duras," *Theatre Journal Staging Gender* 37, no. 3 (1985): 277.

9 Mateusz Borowski and Małgorzata Sugiera, "Political Fictions and Fictionalisations: History as Material for Postdramatic Theatre," in *Postdramatic Theatre and the Political: International Perspectives on Contemporary Performance*, edited by Karen Jürs- Munby, Jerome Carroll and Steve Giles (London and New York: Bloomsbury, 2013), 78.

10 Patterson, *Strategies of Political Theatre,* 19.

11 Ibid.,19.

the spectator."[12] Short movie clips are put together, often to show factual events. "Film clips can be timed to support, expand or comment on the stage action, the images on the stage and on the screens even suggesting cause and effect."[13] Montages are used to highlight the issues Brechtian plays aim to communicate. Narrator tells the audience what is about to happen in the play, before it happens, to prevent them grow intensely emotional about the events. Sometimes actors come out character, often at heightened moments of drama, to remind the audience that it is a piece of fiction that they are watching. "Brecht's stage was to be stripped of its theatrical magic, and the audience refused the state of emotional, empathetic trance."[14] A placard or projection screen can be used to give the audience information about the time of the event; screens are placed "on either side of the stage, upon which were projected photographs of the main characters, together with written summaries of the action in each scene."[15] Actors go into a freeze frame to let the audience stop and think critically for moment, so that the narrator can speak, or so that an actor can come out of character and directly address the audience. "Direct address to the audience would be complete, unlike the traditional hasty aside. Set changes would be made in full view of the audience. In this way stage and audience would be joined, not separated, and speaking directly to the house would be courage."[16] Audience can participate in the play, unlike traditional theatre where they are passive recipients. Actors directly speak to the audience during the performance. Considering the above-mentioned characteristics, Brechtian techniques create political awareness.

In political plays, audience makes a connection between reality and the collective memory. Collective memory provides common knowledge to social group members. It generally occurs at local levels. Each group has a different point of view about their past. Not only their past but also their remembrance and interpretations of the events are different. Thus, collective memory seems a fabricated version of personal memory.[17] Even though each political performance creates its own meaning, the audience's role becomes important since the context changes according to their collective memory. Changing the opinions

12 J. L. Styan, Modern Drama in Theory and Practice 3: Expressionism and Epic Theatre (Cambridge, Cambridge University Press, 1985), 140.

13 Ibid., 131.

14 Ibid., 142.

15 Styan, *Modern Drama in Theory and Practice 3*, 129.

16 Ibid., 143.

17 Noa Gedi and Yigal Elam, "Collective Memory – What Is It?" *History and Memory* 8, no. 1 (1996): 47.

and beliefs of the audience is not easy in political plays. The audience already has collective memory and interprets the performance according to that knowledge. Political plays give the audience the feeling that "they are not alone in their beliefs, that others are actively involved and pursuing the same goals."[18] In other words, postmodernist mode in theatre provides emotional support (patriotism, courage and fighting spirit) to the audience who has already collective memory about the political topics.

Traditional theatre and postmodernist theatre have differences, and the changing role of audience is one of them. Audience becomes more active than before. Brechtian techniques create an opportunity for the audience to participate in the performance. Political awareness of the audience rises due to this method. Subjectivity of the epic theatre does not totally block the political message of the performance. The collective memory of the audience creates emotional and intellectual support. The concept of collective performative memory has always been a core subject in the field of theatre studies as it functions in the way of the audience possessing the memory of specific theatrical and dramatic conventions and in way of appealing to the audience's memory in political remembrances. Recipient's role becomes more important than ever in postmodernist plays. The referential connection of the audience's interaction with the play affects their way of receiving the message and the audience becomes more active due to their own meaning-making process. "The expectations an audience brings to a new reception experience are the residue of memory of previous of such experiences."[19] There is also inclusion of multi-media, and non-verbal theatrical communication between the performer and audience. Collective performative memory engages with the audience's political opinion within a performance. Therefore, performance makes the audience question the subject, though Brecht's way of expressing and criticizing a problem has been different and the style separates itself from the traditional theatre. The interaction between the performer and spectator is an important aspect of the British political plays from 1970s onwards. Breaking the fourth wall in this context allows the actor to communicate directly with the spectator; therefore, it leads the spectator to question the matter at hand. Churchill does not take a side on deciding who is right or wrong in her plays. This is one of the characteristics of modernist plays where the ambiguity and lack of clear resolution in the events inspire the audience to form their own opinions.

---

18 Michael Kirby, "On Political Theatre," The *Drama Review: TDR* 19, no. 2 (1975): 135.
19 Marvin Carlson, The Haunted Stage: The Theatre as Memory Machine (Ann Arbor: University of Michigan Press, 2011), 5.

For this, Churchill includes the Brechtian element of "avoiding catharsis at the end of a production."[20] In her plays there are no clear endings with a specific moral or social lesson, and the interpretation is left to the audience. In the following section, Caryl Churchill's *Cloud Nine* is discussed to illustrate a similar attitude about the subject of patriarchy, changing role of the audience in theatre and the function of collective memory in the formation of the play.

Deconstructing Gender Identity and Patriarchy, Constructing Meaning in *Cloud Nine*

Caryl Churchill is regarded as an important contemporary woman playwright with her unique theatrical expression.[21] She adopts a non-Aristotelian drama and uses Brechtian theatre instead of integrating intellectual audience participation into her plays.[22] She is a critique of patriarchal society and looks for social reformation through her plays. She calls herself, and is referred to, as a socialist feminist because of her approach to contemporary issues in her plays. Referring to contemporary issues, especially gender and identity, in *Cloud Nine*, Churchill uses some theatrical techniques like cross-gender, cross-casting and non-linear narrative, and adopts Butler's gender performativity theory and has a unique characterization of the characters in the play, through which she disrupts the traditional understanding of gender and subverts the authority of patriarchy.

To comprehend Churchill's significance as a contemporary woman playwright, it is necessary to take her social and professional background into consideration. Born in London in 1938, Churchill started her career by writing short stories. Her acceptance to the Royal Court Theatre to work with a group of writers, most of whom were men, during 1960s and 1970s was a milestone in her authorship. Her experiences at the Royal Court influenced

---

20 Alicia Tycer, Caryl Churchill's Top Girls (London: Continuum Books, 2008), 42.

21 In the preface of Mary Luckhurst's Caryl Churchill (London: Routledge, 2014), Caryl Churchill, for her ground-breaking works, "has been internationally celebrated for four decades. She has exploded the narrow definitions of political theatre to write consistently hard-edged and innovative work. Always unpredictable in her stage experiments, her plays have stretched the relationships between form and content, actor and spectator to their limits."

22 In her plays, under the influence of Bertolt Brecht, who argues that "the modern theatre is the epic theatre" (Bertolt Brecht, "The Modern Theatre Is the Epic Theatre: Notes to the Opera," in *Modern Theories of Drama: A Selection of Writings on Drama and Theatre 1850–1990*, edited by George W. Brandt (Oxford: Clarendon, 1998), 227), Churchill deals with gender and sexuality, as a feminist dramatist.

her writing, and inspired from "socialist realist" attitude of those writers, she served for defining the status of women in society with her plays.[23] She criticized the influence of Thatcherism and Margaret Thatcher as a woman prime minister for not improving women's position in society; she was involved in political issues and struggled with patriarchy, prohibiting women freedom of exhibiting their potential of creating and producing for themselves in private and public spheres. In addition to this, "her life as a working mother coincided with the women's movement, and feminist concerns began to influence the content and politics of her plays."[24] Churchill's authorship and theatrical identity were formed within such social, political and family background, and she positioned herself as a contemporary woman playwright at that time with her idiosyncratic ideology and the content of her plays.

Churchill is recognized mostly with her unique theatrical techniques. She is known to have adopted Brechtian theatre and its techniques in her plays. Brechtian epic theatre enhances spectators' reaction during the play's performance and intensifies their role by suggesting that they question the society reflected in the play during the performance and even change it. Brecht strongly proposes that, in modern epic theatre, the emphasis should be on the narrative, rather than the plot, which is a typical of dramatic "old fashioned" theatre.[25] In line with this view, Churchill's *Cloud Nine* begins with a song, which significantly stresses the importance of eloquence within the narrative:

> Come gather, sons of England, come gather in your pride.
> Now meet the world united, now face it side by side;
> Ye who the earth's wide corners, from veldt to prairie, roam.
> From bush and jungle muster all who call old England "home."
> Then gather around for England,
> Rally to the flag,

23 Churchill is known to have worked with other writers, directors, and actors of Joint Stock Theatre Group in a workshop as part of her writing process before she published *Cloud Nine*. Joint Stock Theatre Company's aim is to create the theatre collectively with actors, writers, directors, and other artists in "an attempt to find a more dynamic means of representing revolutionary phenomena." Mary Luckhurst, "On the Challenge of Revolution." The *Cambridge Companion to* Caryl Churchill (Cambridge: Cambridge University Press, 2009), 52–70.

24 Gabrielle H. Cody and Evert Sprinchorn, The *Columbia Encyclopedia of Modern Drama* (New York: Colombia University Press, 2007), 263.

25 Bertolt Brecht, "The Modern Theatre Is the Epic Theatre: Notes to the Opera," in *Modern Theories of Drama: A Selection of Writings on Drama and Theatre 1850–1990*, edited by George W. Brandt (Oxford: Clarendon, 1998), 227.

> From North and South and East and West
> Come one all for England![26]

Rather than explaining in dialogue form the two key terms, patriotism and colonialism, which shape the Victorian era, in which the play is set, Churchill prefers to set the tone with a relatively short song that opens up the play. Clive, Betty, Edward, Victoria, Maud, Ellen, and Joshua are all different characters, each of which stands for a notion, yet they all sing the opening song together, which indicates that they are all united when political concepts are considered. Audience's reaction to what this eight-line song depicts would be different if the idea conveyed by it has been delivered in a dialogue's content between two or more characters. As Judith Butler concludes, the "plot itself is already a shaping of events. What readers in fact encounter is the discourse of a text. If we talk about events that have been shaped into a plot, it is to highlight the meaningfulness and organization of the plot."[27] Accordingly, Churchill makes use of the narrative in the very beginning of the play to give the basic information needed, instead of coming up with a couple of events, which still would not be as revealing as this song, to state the same facts. In postmodern plays, an emphasis on the plot is redundant and it serves no use in performances. Without doubt, since Shakespeare's Globe Theatre – which welcomed all people from different social classes – tastes and expectations of theatregoers have shifted considerably. As Gobert states, "Theatre history is history too, with its own lingering memories and ideologies. Metatheatrically, *Cloud Nine* plays with it: Joshua alludes to blackface minstrelsy, Act 1's Betty to panto camp, Act 2' Cathy (played by a male actor) to the long history of cross-dressed boy actors."[28] The element of homosexuality is integral to the play as it draws attention further into the ideologies during the time of the play's publication. Some critics did not enjoy the inclusion, as they thought it detrimental to Churchill's point. Harding writes "Even in representations that do not involve sex acts, especially if the play purports to subvert the patriarchal constructions of gender, the play's progressive agenda mixes with repressive ideological currents."[29] The characterization of sexuality in her plays is what makes them immersive. Reading or

---

26 All quotes from the text of *Cloud Nine* are from Caryl Churchill, Churchill Plays: One (London and New York: Methuen, 1985), 251.

27 Jonathan D. Culler, Literary Theory: A Very Short Introduction (Oxford: Oxford University Press, 2011), 86.

28 Darren R. Gobert, The Theatre of Caryll Churchill (London: Bloomsbury, 2014), 97.

29 James M. Harding, "Cloud Cover: (Re) Dressing Desire and Comfortable Subversions in Caryl Churchill's Cloud Nine," PMLA 113, no. 2 (1998): 264.

watching the plays makes the audience acknowledge how humans are vulnerable. Therefore, in *Cloud Nine*, Churchill fulfils the expectations of the audience, in the modern sense, Brecht portrays.

As Brechtian theatre addresses social issues and politics about patriarchy, Churchill's plays deal with the issues of gender politics and feminism and support the audience participation in making meaning of the plays' content. She "challenges audiences to join their imaginations with hers in seeking answers to the difficult questions posed by her plays."[30] She is totally against audience passivity and encourages them to speak up in relation to the important issues presented in the plays after questioning them. The type of theatre Churchill acquires enables her to talk about crucial issues like women's status, gender and patriarchy in society freely. In *Cloud Nine*, Churchill comes up with a shift in time, as well as contradictory characters and oppositions in deeds that highlight dichotomies, such as conventional-modern, colonizer-colonized, violence-security, male-female, ruler-ruled and marriage-adultery, to launch an argument regarding the British society. Although themes of her plays resemble those of other contemporary female playwrights like Aphra Behn and Sarah Daniels who write plays in distinct centuries, "her use of theatrical form to alter the relationship between play and audience sets her work apart"[31] and makes her unique.

Another aspect of Churchill's technique is her interest in Butler's idea of gender performativity in *Cloud Nine*. Butler argues that "gender is the repeated stylization of the body, a set of repeated acts within a highly rigid regulatory frame that congeal over time to produce the appearance of substance, of a natural sort of being."[32] Churchill adopts Butler's idea of gender performativity and redefines the notions of femininity and masculinity through her revolutionary construction of characters. Although Churchill is not the first and only woman playwright to have disrupted traditional gender roles with the construction of characters beyond social expectations, her way of applying Butler's theory to her play is peculiar to her. The best example of this is the representation of Edward as a male within social boundaries but as a female inside. He is under the pressure of patriarchy from the beginning mainly because of his father as he insists on

30 Amelia Howe Kritzer, "Theatricality and Empowerment in the Plays of Caryl Churchill," Journal of Dramatic Theory and Criticism 4, no. 1 (1989): 126.

31 Kritzer, "Theatricality and Empowerment in the Plays of Caryl Churchill," 126.

32 Abdol Hossein Joodaki and Paria Bakhshi, "The Collapse of Heterosexism and Phallogocentrism in Caryl Churchill's *Cloud Nine*," *Studies in Literature and Language* 1, no. 6 (2013): 127.

teaching him "to grow up to be a man."[33] Betty and Ellen are displeased with the fact that Edward is playing with dolls, and they try to find excuses for Edward's misbehaviour to prevent Clive from getting angry at Edward, telling him "He's not playing with it. He's minding it for Vicky."[34] Edward keeps displaying feminine manners although Betty warns him, voicing family members' idea that "dolls are for girls,"[35] and that he "must never let the boys at school know [he] like[s] dolls"[36] Edward acts against society's expectations. Churchill embraces Butler's gender performativity and integrates it into her play through characterization of Edward. She comprises Butler's idea that gender "is an assignment which is never quite carried out according to expectation, whose addressee never quite inhabit the ideal s/he is compelled to approximate."[37] She defies conventional codes of society and creates a totally new world in *Cloud Nine*.

Cloud Nine provides a link between Brechtian and post-Brechtian theatre, and the play embodies prominent postmodernist theatrical features with its two-act structure, juxtapositions, doublings of roles and chronological disruption. Churchill's success relies on her intellectual endeavour in exposing socio-cultural and socio-political realities of modern English society. Her ability in combining her theatrical ingenuity with contemporary issues is exemplified in the play's hybrid structure, reverse chronology in cross-acting and cross-dressing. There is a clear distinction between the first and the second act with its audacious time lapse between two. Representation of the characters and the mood of the play drastically changes in the second act. While the setting in the first act is Victorian Africa, the second act takes place in London and although hundred years pass between the acts for the characters it is 25 years late. This sort of disruption in time brings the change in characterization with it because in the second act the characters have more freedom to express their sexual preferences. Churchill exposes how individuals go through a process of exploring their identities and how they can perform their preferred genders when they find the proper conditions of time and space. "A more radical critique of patriarchy comes with the time shift in Act II in which Churchill violates the theatrical convention that character time will be coterminous with the time frame of the text,"[38] which

33 Churchill, Churchill Plays: One, 252.

34 Ibid., 257.

35 Ibid., 274.

36 Ibid., 275.

37 Joodaki, "The Collapse of Heterosexism and Phallogocentrism in Caryl Churchill's *Cloud Nine*," 128.

38 Diamond, "Refusing the Romanticism of Identity," 278.

also turns "the spectator into an observer," making the play in line with another Brechtian feature, due to the fact that "in Act II time has advanced a hundred years but for the characters it is only twenty-five years later. By disturbing diachronic time Churchill lays bare the problematic of history and female identity. No longer the period setting for the zany actions of Act I, the Victorian era can now be read as a set of coded practices that continues to bear pressure on the contemporary characters of Act II."[39] We see Betty embracing the old Betty in the final scene, and this scene renders one of Churchill's theatrical features, inventiveness. She "refuses the finality and closure of stage realism by creating alternative theatrical fictions, parallel universes displaying a different logic and temporal scheme. One of Churchill's means of refusing the closure of representation and the tyranny of the past."[40] Usage of parallel universes creates some comparison and contrast of the characters without separating them as two different things. The past and the present are combined as the past is also part of the character's present.

With all the theatrical innovations in *Cloud Nine*, Churchill's aim is to emphasize "the possibility of the emergence of gender identities who do not match the historically settled and cherished gender categories in the dominant discourse of heterosexuality"[41] and she attempts to "denaturalize and destabilize gender."[42] With her exceptional representations of femininity and masculinity, she "blurs the distinctions between femininity and masculinity"[43] by disrupting the association between the body and the gender. Churchill's approach to gender is distinctive because she manifests "the emptiness and absurdity of such terms as not only feminine and masculine but also the polarized attributes ascribed to femininity and masculinity."[44] Therefore, Churchill has a distinct place in 1970s, 80s with her unique style of turning the perception of gender upside down as an epitome of her consistently innovative dramatic form.

---

39 Ibid.

40 Reinelt, "Beyond Brecht," 186.

41 Joodaki, "The Collapse of Heterosexism and Phallogocentrism in Caryl Churchill's *Cloud Nine*," 129.

42 Ibid., 130.

43 Ibid., 130.

44 Ibid., 131.

Conclusion

Churchill still maintains her significance as a woman playwright. Benedict Nightingale, chief theatre critic for the *Times* (London) and a contributor to the *New York Times* describes her as " 'uniquely important' "[45] due to the fact that "her writing has been greatly influenced by collaborative processes in which she has participated."[46] It is important that for years she has been regarded as "one of only two contemporary women playwrights in the English theatre to receive critical and scholarly attention (the other was Pam Gems)."[47] She is given great attention within politics of literature mostly because "in a world where the writing of women remains under-supported, undervalued, and underproduced, Churchill's work has received widespread critical acclaim and has inspired countless theatre makers but has particularly influenced feminist practitioners and scholars."[48] It has been more than thirty years since *Cloud Nine* was premiered, yet the play manages to be extraordinary and gripping even in today's standards, as well as still having the ability of raising controversy – since it still relates to the major contemporary issues – thanks to Churchill's abolishment of the suppression of sexual feelings, her narrative technique, and noteworthy arguments. The play has been hailed as a major theatrical piece that compels textuality and theatricality. "It was a landmark play in Churchill's repertoire: it confirmed her as a major, innovative, and political dramatist in British theatre, and brought her to international attention when, in 1981, the play transferred to New York where it ran for two years."[49] *Cloud Nine* provides a reading in transition from Brechtian to post-Brechtian and to postmodernist theatre with Churchill's groundbreaking presentation of fringe drama. Rather than redefining sexual politics in the play, Churchill suggests that sexual orientations and tendencies cannot be categorized and repressed.

Cloud Nine is written in a distinctive structure and the play's cast is required to cross-dress and role-play as each other, the play itself is oriented according to the identities of a Victorian household in the first act, as their identities are questioned and replaced, challenging the restraints of social constructs of society

45 Cody and Sprinchorn, The *Columbia Encyclopedia of Modern Drama*, 262.

46 Ibid., 264.

47 Elaine Aston, *Feminist Views on* the *English Stage: Women Playwrights, 1990–2000* (New York: Cambridge University Press, 2003), 18.

48 Gabrielle H. Cody and Evert Sprinchorn. The *Columbia Encyclopedia of Modern Drama*. (New York: Colombia University Press , 2007), 263.

49 Gobert, The Theatre of Caryll Churchill, 209.

reflected in individuals. Restraints of social structure is contested and criticized through the individuals in society. All the above stated questionings and deflations are corresponding with what postmodernism stands for. As Darren Gobert states in his analysis of Caryl Churchill's theatre, "she turned to the question of how the body is shaped not only by self-concepts but also by the social and ideological contexts that condition its material expression: contexts that tell a boy to carry himself in this manner or a woman to sit down in that. Churchill's play theatricalizes how the body expresses the weight of its historical burdens as it adapts to fit a role predetermined by ideological pressures."[50] One can see the mirrored ideals of postmodernism in Churchill's theatre, which opposes traditional concepts and instead calls for ambitious and stylized writings in opposition to modernism.

Cloud Nine has its unique place in Churchill's repertory vis-à-vis deconstructing social expectations and challenging the identities that are assigned to and held upon the individuals to adopt. Characters in *Cloud Nine* often lose their identity and change characteristics, which is also required of the play's cast to be performed. They push the boundaries of identity and what it means to be a person without the constraints of societal norms and regulations. This, too, is related to postmodernism that confers Churchill's writing style to compel the boundaries of conventional narratives.

Bibliography

Aston, Elaine. *Feminist Views on the English Stage: Women Playwrights, 1990–2000*. New York: Cambridge University Press, 2003.

Brecht, Bertolt. "The Modern Theatre Is the Epic Theatre: Notes to the Opera." In *Modern Theories of Drama: A Selection of Writings on Drama and Theatre 1850–1990*, edited by George W. Brandt. Oxford: Clarendon, 1998, 224–231.

Borowski, Mateusz, and Małgorzata Sugiera. "Political Fictions and Fictionalisations: History as Material for Postdramatic Theatre." In *Postdramatic Theatre and the Political: International Perspectives on Contemporary Performance*, edited by Karen Jürs-Munby, Jerome Carroll, and Steve Giles. London and New York: Bloomsbury, 2013: 67–86.

Carlson, Marvin. *The Haunted Stage: The Theatre as Memory Machine*. Ann Arbor: University of Michigan Press, 2011.

Churchill, Caryl. *Churchill Plays: One*. London and New York: Methuen, 1985.

50 Ibid., 85.

Cody, Gabrielle H., and Evert Sprinchorn. *The Columbia Encyclopedia of Modern Drama*. New York: Colombia University Press, 2007.

Culler, Jonathan D. "Narrative." In *Literary Theory: A Very Short Introduction*. Oxford: Oxford University Press, 2011, 83–94.

Diamond, Elin. "Refusing the Romanticism of Identity: Narrative Interventions inChurchill, Benmussa, Duras." *Theatre Journal Staging Gender* 37, no. 3 (1985): 273–286. https://www.jstor.org/stable/3206848.

Gedi, Noa, and Yigal Elam. "Collective Memory – What Is It?" *History and Memory* 8, no. 1 (1996): 30–50. https://www.jstor.org/stable/pdf/25618696.pdf.

Gobert, R. Darren. *The Theatre of Caryll Churchill*. London: Bloomsbury, 2014.

Harding, James M. "Cloud Cover: (Re) Dressing Desire and Comfortable Subversions in Caryl Churchill's Cloud Nine." *PMLA* 113, no. 2 (1998): 258–272.

Harlow, Lauren. "The Misconception of Memory: Part One." *St. Luke's Historic Church & Museum*. Accessed 15 January 2021. https://stlukesmuseum.org/misconception-memory-hsl-2-2/.

Joodaki, Abdol Hossein, and Paria Bakhshi. "The Collapse of Heterosexism and Phallogocentrism in Caryl Churchill's *Cloud Nine*." *Studies in Literature and Language* 1, no. 6 (2013): 127–131. DOI: 10.3968/j.sll.1923156320130601.3105

Keyssar, Helene. "The Dramas of Caryl Churchill: The Politics of Possibility." *The Massachusetts Review* 24, no. 1 (1983): 198–216.

Kirby, Michael. "On Political Theatre." *The Drama Review: TDR* 19, no. 2 (1975): 129–135. https://www.jstor.org/stable/1144954.

Kritzer, Amelia Howe. "Theatricality and Empowerment in the Plays of Caryl Churchill." *Journal of Dramatic Theory and Criticism* 4, no. 1 (1989): 125–131.

Luckhurst, Mary. "On The Challenge of Revolution." In *The Cambridge Companion to Caryl Churchill*, edited by Elaine Aston and Elin Diamond. New York: Cambridge University Press, 2009. https://www.cambridge.org/core/books/cambridge-companion-to-caryl-churchill/on-the-challenge-of-revolution/1E0E7CBC92A31ABBCF2135E384933F0C.

Luckhurst, Mary. "Preface." In *Caryl Churchill*. London: Routledge, 2014, 1–23

Malkin, Jeanette R. *Memory-Theatre and Postmodern Drama*. Ann Arbor : The University of Michigan Press, 1999.

Patterson, Michael. *Strategies of Political Theatre: Post-War British Playwrights*. Cambridge: Cambridge University Press, 2003.

Reinelt, Janelle. "Beyond Brecht: Britain's New Feminist Drama." *Theatre Journal* 38, no. 2 (1986): 154–163. https://www.jstor.org/stable/3208116.

Šešić, Milena Dragićević, and Milena Stefanović. "How Theaters Remember: Cultures of Memory in Institutionalized Systems." *Култура/Culture* 24, no. 4 (2014): 11–30. https://journals.cultcenter.net/index.php/culture/article/view/72.

Styan, J. L., *Modern Drama in Theory and Practice 3: Expressionism and Epic Theatre*. Cambridge: Cambridge University Press, 1985.

Tycer, Alicia. *Caryl Churchill's Top Girls*. London: Continuum Books, 2008.

Mesut Günenç

Deciphering Postdramatic Tragedy in Sarah Kane's *Phaedra's Love*

Introduction

In western cultural tradition and traditional form of dramatic conception, imitation, the text, chorus, and singing were vital elements. These vital elements date back to the time of Aristotle and his work *Poetics* which aims to establish "the hierarchy of the elements – mythos (plot), character, dianoia (thought) and speech."[1] Parallel to Aristotle's notions, Hans Thies Lehmann explains (tragic) drama as follows: "action of a superior kind-grand, and complete in itself-presented in embellished language, in distinct forms in different parts, performed by actors rather than told by a narrator, effecting, through pity and fear, the purification of such emotions."[2] The soul of dramatic tragedy (mimesis and the logos of a totality) covers the Roman tradition adding with rhetorical discussion five act form and thought of revenge with bloody scenes. Thought of traditional drama traces back through Renaissance to second half of seventeenth and eighteenth centuries, and narration, form of unity, and well-organized structure have acted till second half of the nineteenth century. To the end of nineteenth century, new theatrical practices have been started to observe, closing bound with the textuality and logos of the totality have been disrupted. New meaning has been given to theatre through distinctive advancements in society and art. By the help of avant-garde movements and using of new elements, scenographic transformation has occurred. The fourth wall of the traditional/naturalist/realist theatre was demolished and the play has been open to audiences' interpretation. Experi(m)ential theatrical model arose in an attempt to step away from the ostensibly obsolete dramatic model.[3]

New developments and Brecht's Epic Theatre, portraying alienation effect and bringing social realities (his fable) to the surface, shape non-dramatic

1 Hans Thies Lehmann, "From Logos to Landscape: Text in Contemporary Dramaturgy," *Perfromance Research* (2015), 55.

2 Hans Thies Lehmann, *Postdramatic Theatre* (Translated by Karen Jürs-Munby. Abingdon: Routledge, 2006), 40.

3 Patrice Pavis, *Dictionary of the Theatre: Terms, Concepts, and Analysis* (Toronto: University of Toronto Press, 1998), 120.

performance. Lehmann, exploring theatrical practices in the 1960s and 1970s, traces the historical process of postdramatic theatre and tragedy:

> The "take off" wards a formation of postdramatic discourse in theatre can be described as a series of stages of self-reflection, decomposition and separation of the elements of dramatic theatre. The path leads from the grand theatre at the end of the nineteenth century, via a multitude of modern theatre forms during the historical avant-garde and then the neo-avant garde of the 1950s and 1960s, to the postdramatic theatre forms at the end of the twentieth and the beginning of the twenty first centuries.[4]

Concepts of theatre and artistic forms have experienced reformist change reflecting state of the life in every moment of history. Starting from verbally active participation in the sixteenth century until Brecht's thought of participation to the performance in Epic Theatre, the aim of the theatre was to move audience, to prevent callousness and insouciance. That desire goes on in-yer-face theatre, and in the 1990s, performances presented obscene language, shocking themes and portrayal of violence and sex onstage. The ending of the twentieth century and the beginning of the twenty-first century illustrate a new and experimental style as postdramatic text and tragedy.

Postdramatic tragedy is the reinvention and adaptation of the ancient tragedy. By the help of classical concepts, texts can be divided into dramatic and postdramatic categories, like a palimpsest, texts represent a legacy and dramatic origins.[5] Lehmann himself defines "palimpsestuous intertextuality and intratextuality a significant characteristic of much postdramatic theatre."[6] Approaching Lehmann's thought and analyzing postmodern terms as intertextuality and intratextuality, a dichotomizing relation between dramatic and postdramatic text can be combined. Postdramatic theatre is called an anamnesis of dramatic theatre[7] and differences between dramatic and postdramatic text do not indicate a binary opposition:

> The distinction between dramatic and postdramatic-which is not a binary opposition in any event, but a dynamic relationship in which the postdramatic continues to engage with the dramatic-cannot be reduced to such distinctions as "text-based" versus "non-text-based" (avant-garde) theatre, or "verbal" versus "physical" theatre, as Lehmann himself stresses.[8]

---

4 Lehmann, *Postdramatic Theatre*, 48.
5 Emma Cole, *Postdramatic Tragedies* (Oxford: Oxford University Press, 2019), 36
6 Lehmann, *Postdramatic Theatre*, 7.
7 Karen Juers Munby, Introduction Part in *Postdramatic Theatre*, 2.
8 Munby, "Jelinek[Jahr]buch" (Annual publication of the Elfriede Jelinek Reserearch Centre Janke, P. (ed.). Vienna: Praesens Verlag, 2011), 86.

Contrary to these explanations, selecting, revising and adapting the text from ancient tragedies, postdramatic theatre goes beyond dramatic theatre by deconstructing dramatic form. Dramatic form and representations have intensely changed in the postdramatic period. Postdramatic text adopts a great variety of formats and techniques. "Next to the continued interest in the expressive possibilities of the written word, numerous other modes of representations (such as drawings, sketches, videos, lists, Dropbox files, score, annotations, diagrams, etc.) have become, arguably more than ever, vital means of theatrical creation."[9] Deconstruction of dramatic form and experi(m)ential performances can be observed in Sarah Kane, one of the most idiosyncratic playwrights of Contemporary British Drama. Kane's works contains tragic feelings and postdramatic constitution. Her last play *4.48 Psychosis* is identified as "one of the strongest contemporary examples of tragic text."[10] In Kane's plays, tragic moments are portrayed and generated by violent, depressive, suicidal, and psychotic factors which force audiences to become active witnesses who are able to produce meaning and evaluate the performance. The other experi(m)ential performance *Phaedra's Love*, bearing witness to tragic side of postdramatic theatre and changing the perception of each other, represents more rapeful and disordered structure than dramatic form. The study analyses *Phaedra's Love* drawing pointedly from the work of one of the distinctive contemporary British playwrights Sarah Kane and the theory of Hans Thies Lehmann's postdramatic theatre and his discussion on postdramatic tragedy.

Sarah Kane

Sarah Kane, who emerged in British theatre in the last part of the twentieth century, is one of the distinctive writers who push the boundaries of traditional theatre the most. On the other hand, the most notorious playwright in Britain Sarah Kane, who committed suicide on February 1999 at the age of 28, fits into her short but contradictory life an irregular and experi(m)ential theatre life because she is apprehensive of the power of the theatre; thus, she "risks an overdose in theatre than in life."[11] By the help of theatre, Kane speaks to us most deeply. Kane

9 Timmy De Leat Cassiers and Luk Van Den Dries, "Text: The Director's Notebook," in *Postdramatic Theatre and Form*, edited by Michael Shane Boyle, Matt Cornish and Brandon Woolf (London: Bloomsbury, 2019), 33.

10 Lehmann, T*ragedy and Dramatic Theatre* (London: Routledge, 2016), 436.

11 Graham Saunders, *Love Me or Kill Me: Sarah Kane and the Theatre of Extremes*, (Manchester: Manchester University Press, 2002), 22.

wrote only five plays during her twenty-eight years life; however, her plays have ensured and will always keep her as a young and contemporary playwright in British theatre. Kane, one of the children of Thatcher era, who is affected by the socio-political structure and harsh rules of the period and who is stated to be in "in-yer-face perception," uses the themes of sex, violence, nudity, war, rape and rough language. Like her colleagues, Kane nevertheless rejects the label and movement:

> I do not believe in movements. Movements define retrospectively and always on grounds of imitation [. . .] the writers themselves are not interested in it. Some of the writers who are said to belong to the [in-yer-face] movement I haven't even met. So, as far as I am concerned, I hope that my play is not typical of anything.[12]

With her five plays *Blasted*, *Phaedra's Love*, *Cleansed*, *Crave*, and *4.48 Psychosis*, Kane herself formed the movement which disrupts the convention and boundaries of dramatic theatre and tragedy. "Refusing to follow a structural order, she instead prefers the marriage of opposites in her plays: emotional complexity expressed through linguistic concision, obscure stage imagery embellished with moments of clarity and lyricism coupled with acts of cruelty."[13] Kane is also harshly criticized because she rejects existing traditional maxims and presents shocking scenes, including elements such as sex, abuse, torture, persecution and cannibalism in her plays. The author, representing problematic, disruptive and political themes and deconstructing dramatic structure of tragedy, writes her text mainly for performance which can be accepted as postdramatic tragedy. Within the context of historical period, ancient tragedy is the source of modern tragedy and represents public issues, politics, power, confliction and violence through different ages. Lehmann claims that the concept of tragedy is basically political, as it is connected to public issues of history, power and conflict, and puts basic cultural assumptions at risk.

The themes and the structure in Kane's plays conform to Lehmann's definition of tragic mode. For that reason, as Aristotle defines Sophocles' *Oedipus the Rex* as the best tragedy that fits the dramatic structure, Lehmann describes Kane's plays and *4.48 Psychosis* in particular, as the definitive examples of postdramatic text. Actually, Kane's works represent to the examples of significant tragedies and are generally associated with classical sensitivity. Kane's debut *Blasted* (1995)

---

12 Saunders, *Love Me or Kill Me*, 7.

13 Yeliz Biber Vangölü, "Sarah Kane's *Cleansed* as a Critical Assessment of Disciplinary Power", *Ankara University the Journal of the Faculty of Languages and History-Geography*, 57, no. 1 (2017): 275.

make references to *Oedipus the Rex* and Shakespeare's Jacobean tragedy *King Lear*. Kane, removing Ian's eyes, brings to mind both gouging of Oedipus' and Gloucester's eyes. The combination of Shakespearean referents (*Titus Andronicus*) with classic allusions, Kane's play *Cleansed* represents tragic elements (pain and catharsis) with postdramatic techniques. "Each of her five plays engages conceptually with ideas of the tragic and infuses a politicized, post-Thatcher sensibility with images and plot devices from the classical canon."[14] Demonstrating her mastery of adapting distinctive tragedies in the past to the modern era, Kane reveals the relationship between postdramatic techniques and the tragic aspects in *Phaedra's Love*.

Tragic Aspects in *Phaedra's Love*

Inspired by the story of Phaedra in mythology, "Kane's play takes the skeleton of Seneca's story (and that of Euripides before him),"[15] Büchner's *Woyzeck* and Brecht's play *Baal*, *Phaedra's Love* has been staged at Gate Theatre on 15 May 1996 after the "Kane's the biggest theatrical stir."[16] Staged in a contemporary adaptation, the play, a contemporary response, also presents influences from the tragedies of the seventeenth and eighteenth centuries:

> *Phaedra's Love* not only retains the tragic protagonist from Seneca's classical Roman drama, but its bloody climax also transposes elements from Elizabethan and Jacobean revenge tragedy, in which a form of staged violence is performed that is both outlandish and shocking to the sensibilities.[17]

In *Phaedra's Love*, Kane deconstructing original structure of the myth reshapes it to conditions of Britain in the 1990s. Kane's interpretation is different from Seneca's *Phaedra* in which "Hippolytus was chaste and morally virtuous. Kane's is not."[18] Kane, adding experimental interpretation and sharing space with audience, form a new performance.

The play is bound up with the theme of love, which even has an inhuman side, and with an irrepressible sexual desire. The play hones in more on Phaedra's

---

14 Cole, *Postdramatic Tragedies*, 47.

15 Elizabeth Barry, "'Conscious Sin': Seneca, Sarah Kane and The Apprasisal of Emotion," *Canadian Review of Comparative Literature* (2013), 123.

16 Kate Basset. Rev. of Phaedra"s Love, by Sarah Kane. Dir. Kane, The Gate Theatre, Notting Hill. 20 May–15 June (1996), *The Times*, 22 May 1996.

17 Saunders, *Love Me or Kill Me*, 80.

18 Ian Ward. "Rape and Rape Mythology in the Plays of Sarah Kane." *Comparative Drama* 47, no. 47.2 (2013): 235.

stepson Hippolytus, a self-centred and rotted prince, eating junk food, masturbating into a sock, having random sex both with women and men, whose life is meaningless and all thoughts are an agonizing threat. Jaded Hippolytus was the main character of the play. Contrary to Seneca's masterpiece, the brutality deciphered in *Phaedra's Love* is embodied in performance. When Kane reads Seneca's Phaedra, she is struck by the existence of a sexually corrupted royal family and the protagonist Hippolytus being highly repulsive due to his simple, bigoted, and human-hating personality.[19] The play revolves around Phaedra's obsession with her stepson Hippolytus, the path that this love ultimately leads to her suicide and acts of violence, and the terrifying punishment imposed on her dead body by her husband Theseus. Kane creates the contemporary Phaedra by addressing the issues of social breakdown, power ambition, sexual deviance, love, savagery, and violence, and adapting ancient tragedy to twentieth century capitalist society.

Kane highlights the violence in the ancient story and presents it to audience at the end of the twentieth century. Through *Phaedra's Love*, Kane also seeks to reflect how contemporary societies and the capitalist system alienate people from each other, leaving them purposeless and rootless. Within this context, Aleks Sierz calls the play as "the dialogue veers from exchanges that are genuinely disturbing to such boneheaded declarations as 'Fuck God; fuck the monarchy.'"[20] Samantha Marlowe, for experi(m)ential structure of the play, clarifies that

> The boundaries between audience and actors are deliberately blurred – there is no single playing space, and the seating is dispersed so that involvement is unavoidable. Not that you would want to avoid it, when there is so much going on that's too good to miss. Sexual hunger, hypocrisy, rape, suicide – it's all uncompromisingly here, but in a manner that somehow avoided deteriorating into lurid voyeurism.[21]

Kane's production *Phaedra's Love* produces a complex and visceral structure which forces spectators to answer physically. On the other hand, Kane wants to reword the story of Phaedra to cross the borders of dramatic performances by representing her audience how ancient tragedies are unenthusiastic to stage. Forming relations with Seneca's tragic elements such as sexuality, violence, politics and voyeurism, Kane's *Phaedra's Love* creates a postdramatic recognition on

---

19 Aleks Sierz, *In-Yer-Face Theatre: British Drama Today* (London: Faber and Faber, 2001), 139.

20 Aleks Sierz, rev. of Phaedra"s Love, by Sarah Kane, dir. Kane, The Gate Theatre, Notting Hill, Tribune, 20 May–15 June 1996.

21 Samantha Marlow, "Phaedra's Love," *Theatre Record* 16 (1996): 652.

audience. Emma Cole clarifies experi(m)ential role of audience and function of Gate theatre:

> The Gate's tiny theatre, which seats less than one hundred spectators, combined with the quasi-immersive seating arrangement to create a postdramatic space, meaning that the physical and physiological proximity of the actors to the spectators evoked a theatre of shared energies rather than transmitted signs.[22]

Creating a postdramatic space and seating actors among spectators make spectators to question whether this is a part of the play or a fictional act. This action also refers to "irruption of the real," one of the postdramatic theatrical signs of Lehmann. Spectators start to question fictional side of the play and the reality and try to deconstruct boundaries between themselves and the stage through theatrical sign "Irruption of the real," which "implicitly invites not only performative acts that confer new meanings but also such performative acts that bring about meaning in a new way, or rather: put meaning itself at stake."[23]

The first scene of the play focuses on Hippolytus, who sits idly in a dark room, lingers with expensive electronic toys and watches a Hollywood-made violent movie while eating chips under a blanket. Unlike classical texts, the author, who does not include dialogues, presents a postdramatic example of space by including media tools. Through media tools and without dialogue, spectators try to create their own logic from Hippolytus's performance and understand temporality phenomenon which asks for new consideration from spectators. Dramatic logic, using linear structure, is deconstructed in *Phaedra's Love* because of Hippolytus's inertia. On the other hand, media and television on the stage create a metaphorical language which supports Lehmann's thought: "the body in theatre is a signifier (not the object) of desire. The electronic image, by contrast, is pure foreground. It evokes a fulfilled, superficially fulfilled kind of seeing."[24] The spectators, who witness the individual who is unconcerned with the media's news of rape and murder and the bodies tortured (Hippolytus), committed suicide (Phaedra) and raped (Strophe), are disturbed by the method of density of signs and are incorporated in the play. Through postdramatic practice "density of signs," spectators are forced to witness sexual and physical violence and solve the confliction between reality and fiction. Kane's experiential performance aims to create connection with spectator and physicality and as in postdramatic theatre, this performance needs making meaning and active participation.

---

22 Cole, *Postdramatic Tragedies*, 51.
23 Lehmann, *Postdramatic Theatre*, 102.
24 Ibid., 171.

Like the classical one that presents the conversation between Phaedra and Nurse, the second scene of the play includes a conversation between Phaedra, worried about Hippolytus' state of health, with the doctor who is summoned to the palace to correct Hippolytus condition. After making initial diagnosis of Hippolytus' condition, Doctor questions Phaedra's feelings about her stepson: "Does he have sex with you?" and "Are you in love with him,"[25] Phaedra responds with no persuasive statements: "I'm his stepmother. We are royal" and "I'm married to his father."[26] Like the Nurse who systematically tries to warn Phaedra and her feelings about Hippolytus, Doctor stating "Get over him"[27] warns Phaedra about Hippolytus.

Scene three of the play represents the conversation between Phaedra and her daughter Strophe. Hippolytus is undoubtedly on Phaedra's agenda and accepts her incestuous desire. Strophe, who has made love with Hippolytus before, tries to defame Hippolytus and keep Phaedra off him:

Phaedra: You tired of Hippolytus.
Strophe: He bores me.
Phaedra: Bores you?
Strophe: Shitless.
Phaedra: Why Everyone likes him.
Strophe: I know.
Phaedra: I know what room he's in.
(…)
Strophe: Why don't you have an affair, get your mind off him.
(…)
Strophe: He's twenty years younger than you.
Phaedra: Want to climb inside him work out.[28]

Despite Strophe's warnings, Phaedra cannot deny her desires and goes to Hippolytus's room and begs him to sleep with her in Scene four. It is observed that all the borders of Phaedra have disappeared in scene four. Phaedra also reveals her own passion by bringing a gift to Hippolytus in order to express herself and communicate:

Phaedra: Have you ever thought about having sex with me?
Hippolytus: I think about having sex with everyone.
Phaedra: Would it make you happy?

25 Sarah Kane, *Complete Plays* (London: Methuen, 2001), 66–67.
26 Ibid., 66–67.
27 Ibid., 68.
28 Ibid., 70–71.

Hippolytus: That's not the word exactly.
(…)
Phaedra: Then why do it?
Hippolytus: Life's too long.
(…)
Phaedra: I'm in love with you.[29]

Phaedra unfastens Hippolytus's pant and performs oral sex on him, knowing that Hippolytus will not have sexual intercourse with her. Because of this behaviour, Phaedra is no different to Hippolytus from other women. Phaedra is one of those women he slept with to spend his day. Phaedra insistently telling Hippolytus how passionate her love is, however, Phaedra's begging for love has no meaning for Hippolytus. Phaedra reminds Hippolytus of the trauma he experienced in the past by mentioning the character Lena, who is presented as unidentified, to Hippolytus:

Hippolytus: No one burns me.
Phaedra: What about that woman?
Hippolytus: What?
Phaedra: Lena, weren't you-
Hippolytus: (Grabs Phaedra by the throat.)
Don't ever mention her again.
Don't say her name to me, don't refer to
Her, don't even think about her, understand?
Understand?.[30]

The character Lena, who emerged as the source of trauma and depression, can be portrayed as a girlfriend or mother figure who messed up Hippolytus. Thereupon, Hippolytus, saying "See a doctor. I've got gonorrhea"[31] insults Phaedra and his past relations as if in revenge. With these disastrous words in the fourth scene, the process of extinction of the characters in the text emerges, at the same time the fourth wall is deconstructed by showing the pain on the stage and the experiential performance emerges.

Scene five started with a dialogue between Strophe and Hippolytus. Upon the death of Phaedra, who accused Hippolytus of raping her and thus committed suicide, Strophe antagonizes Hippolytus about her mother's suicide. However, her love for Hippolytus, as well as the thought that if she killed Hippolytus,

29 Ibid., 79–80.
30 Ibid., 82–83.
31 Ibid., 85.

prevents Strophe from achieving her purpose. She tries to persuade Hippolytus, insisting that he did not rape Phaedra, but to speak the truth and resist:

Strophe:	Tell me you didn't rape her.
Hippolytus:	Love me?
Strophe:	Tell me you didn't do it.
Hippolytus:	She says I did and she's dead. Believe her. Easier all around.
Strophe:	What is wrong with you?
Hippolytus:	This is her present to me.[32]

The pain and suicide of Phaedra will be the catharsis of the Hippolytus. The death of Phaedra means purification and a new beginning for Hippolytus. Hippolytus, complaining about the meaninglessness of life and depicting his future sentence and death as the chance he has been longing for a long time, chooses to die.

In the following scene, Hippolytus starts to discuss with the priest instead of Strophe. The priest advises Hippolytus to confess lying about ravishing his stepmother and to give up the thought of suicide. They also address the role of God and the essence of sin; however, it is not easy for the priest to argue with Hippolytus who does not believe in God or does not want to accept the last minute help from God:

Hippolytus:	What do you suggest, a last minute conversion just in case? Die as if there is a God, knowing that there isn't? No. If there is a God, I'd like to look him in the face knowing I'd died as I'd lived. In conscious sin.
(...).	
Priest:	Pray with me. Save yourself. And your country. Don't commit that sin.[33]

However, the priest's efforts were in vain. Hippolytus does not want to be forgiven and "asserts a philosophy of living by a creed of absolute honesty"[34] the scene ends with Hippolytus's words:

> It may be enough for you, but I have no intention of covering my arse. I killed a woman and I will be punished for it by hypocrites who I shall take down with me. May we burn in hell. God may be all powerful, but there's one thing he can't do.[35]

Scene seven presents Phaedra's funeral pyre and Theseus who finds out that Hippolytus has raped Phaedra and goes mad. Stating that he will kill

---

32 Ibid., 90.

33 Ibid., 94–95.

34 Graham Saunders, *About Kane: the Playwright and the Work* (London: Faber and Faber, 2009), 22.

35 Kane, *Complete Plays*, 98.

Hippolytus: "I'll kill him"[36] Theseus's words are actually an expression that everyone's end is soon.

The final scene of the play portrays the annihilation of the royal family. Disguised Strophe and Theseus, who get into the crowd, wait Hippolytus' trial. Hippolytus is lynched by Theseus and agitated crowded, his head crushed with stones and sticks, and his penis amputated. In this scene of brutality, Strophe among the crowds tries to defend Hippolytus, however, is raped by his bloodthirsty stepfather Theseus for her true identity is not known. Theseus, after learning the truth and losing all his loved ones, in his guilt, slitting his own throat commits suicide.

From the very beginning of the play, the brutality is conveyed to the audience both on the stage and through visual dramaturgy. Kane also makes thousands of people watch the murder of Hippolytus on television. In other words, Kane continues the dialectical relations by the help of postdramatic technique, density of signs. The most distinctive scene of *Phaedra's Love* represents riot, rape, blood, murder and cannibalism which take place in and among audiences by the help of density of images. Kane's dialectical performance reflects Lehmann's global perception (synaesthesia) which determines rediscovery in the text.[37] On the other hand, postdramatic stage space, which represents suffering bodies on stage, bodies, gestures, signs and movements, shapes postdramatic language which creates "scenic poem."[38] As a scenic poem, Kane's text is chained with physicality of the actors for that reason audiences cannot escape from eye contact and physical closeness. Within this physical concept, last scene in the play portraying the putrefaction of a human being that is currently occurring on stage reveals the staging process of pain and purification. The play embodies postdramatic pain and body in postdramatic theatre:

> When the stage is becoming like life, when people really fall or really get hit on stage, the spectators start to fear for the players. The novelty resides in the fact that there is a transition from represented pain to pain experienced in representation.[39]

Exhibition of the body and violence on the stage define Sarah Kane's experimental performance. "Experiential is the reference point Kane herself used for the theatre she wanted to make … It is a theatre that must be lived through."[40]

---

36 Ibid.

37 Lehmann, *Postdramatic Theatre*, 85.

38 Ibid., 110.

39 Ibid., 166.

40 Clare Wallace, "Sarah Kane, Experiential Theatre and the Revenant Avant-garde," in *Sarah Kane in Context*, edited by L. de Vos and G. Saunders (Manchester and New York: Manchester University Press, 2010), 89.

Her performance creates sensation of danger on the audience because audience observes violence and the scene of anarchism. Kane intends to "break down the barriers between audience and the actors where seating was dispersed around the theatre, and no single playing space selected."[41] The play forms direct physical contact with thoughts and disrupt the boundaries between reality and fiction which had already started to combine the positions of the audiences and the performers, and it deconstructs the obligation of the audiences for the theatrical performance that they can co-create the performance by their thoughts, behaviours and participation.[42] Each audience watching the murder of Hippolytus is actually the audience who is indifferent to the violence, pain, rape and destruction around them and the audience's responsibility must be maximized during the performance.

Conclusion

Operating several postdramatic techniques, Kane portrays violence as the central theme to audiences. While representing the audience, Kane especially uses shared space and retreat from synthesis techniques of postdramatic theatre which aggravates a direct relation with the concept of violence by provoking the audience through a series of disconcerting images and metaphor which support the thought as the need for an open and fragmenting experience as opposed to a cohesive and closed awareness is evident in postdramatic theatre.[43] Lehmann creates a new mimetic understanding, which operates the mimetic presenters connect with the audience. Instead of a simple representation, density of signs illustrates the performance. In the play, violent and sexual acts are represented through density of signs and deconstruct unifying perception and comprehensible performance because "provocation in the theatre finds its locus in the space between stage and audience, blurring and infringing on the protection offered by the representation, thus bridging the abyss and filling in the moat. It does this mainly by pulling the spectator into the dramatic conversation that takes place on the stage."[44] Kane hones in on that audience's protection is to

41 Graham Saunders, "'If There Could Have Been More Moments Like This': Phaedra's Love," in *Sarah Kane in Context* (Manchester: Manchester University Press 2010).

42 Lehmann, *Postdramatic Theatre*, 124.

43 Ibid., 82.

44 Piet Defraeye, "In-Yer-Face Theatre? Reflections on Provocation and Provoked Audiences in Contemporary Theatre," in *Extending the Code: New Forms of Dramatic and Theatrical Expression*, edited by Hans-Ulrich Mohr and Kerstin Machler (Contemporary Drama in English 11. Trier: WVT, 2004): 81.

be disrupted when the provocation occurs and audience's safe zone is disturbed. The idea of provocation does not mean to push away the audience; on the contrary it is telling the truth to the audience for that reason audience is positioned as accomplice to violence and responsible to resolve the problem which is shared by performers and audiences. The role of the audience and the purpose of shared space in theatre are defined by Lehmann as:

> Quietly radicalizes the responsibility of the spectators for the theatrical process, which they can co-create but also disturb or even destroy through their behaviour. The vulnerability of the process becomes its raison d'être and inquires into the norms of everyday behaviour.[45]

Like Lehmann, Kane, emphasizing the importance of the audience's responsibility, forces the audience to recognize their own capacity and to learn what happens in the contemporary world. "In *Phaedra's Love* the symbiotic relationship between postdramatic techniques and classical tragedy represents an indicative instance of how text and postdramatic techniques worked hand in hand rather than in opposition during 1990s British theatre."[46] Kane tries to form the bridge between Senecan times and themes with experi(m)ential techniques in contemporary time. Extended perception of the postdramatic tragedy refers to the concept of reworked, adapted and modified text decline the importance of dramatic perception. Kane actually intends to portray the conventional concepts of ancient theatre such as love, brutality, death, revenge and suicide, at the same time represents an entirely contemporary tragedy.

Bibliography

Barry, Elizabeth. "'Conscious Sin': Seneca, Sarah Kane and the Appraisal of Emotion." *Canadian Review of Comparative Literature,* 40, no.1 (2013): 122–135.

Basset, Kate. Review of Phaedra's Love, by Sarah Kane. Dir. Kane, The Gate Theatre, Notting Hill. 20 May to 15 June (1996), *The Times,* 22 May 1996.

Cassiers, Timmy De Leat and Dries, Luk Van Den. "Text: The Director's Notebook." In *Postdramatic Theatre and Form*, edited by Michael Shane Boyle, Matt Cornish, and Brandon Woolf, 33–47. London: Bloomsbury, 2019.

Cole, Emma. *Postdramatic Tragedies.* Oxford: Oxford University Press, 2019.

45 Lehmann, *Postdramatic Theatre*, 124.
46 Cole, *Postdramatic Tragedies*, 47.

Defraeye, Piet. "In-Yer-Face Theatre? Reflections on Provocation and Provoked Audiences in Contemporary Theatre." In *Extending the Code: New Forms of Dramatic and Theatrical Expression. Contemporary Drama in English* 11, edited by Hans-Ulrich Mohr and Kerstin Machler, 79–97. Trier: WVT, 2004.

Juers-Munby, Karen. Jelinek[Jahr]buch (Annual publication of the Elfriede Jelinek Research Centre). Edited by Janke, P., 85–102. Vienna: Praesens Verlag, 2011.

Juers-Munby, Karen. "Introduction." In *Postdramatic Theatre*, 1–15 Abingdon: Routledge, 2006.

Kane, Sarah. *Complete Plays*. London: Methuen, 2001.

Lehmann, Hans Thies. *Postdramatic Theatre*. Translated by Karen Jürs-Munby. Abingdon: Routhledge, 2006.

Lehmann, Hans Thies. "From Logos to Landscape: Text in Contemporary Dramaturgy." *Performance Research*, 2, no.1 (2015): 55–60.

Marlow, Samantha. "Phaedra's Love." *Theatre Record*, 16 (1996): 652.

Pavis, Patrice. *Dictionary of the Theatre: Terms, Concepts, and Analysis*. Toronto: University of Toronto Press, 1998.

Saunders, Graham. *Love Me or Kill Me: Sarah Kane and the Theatre of Extremes*. Manchester: Manchester University Press, 2002.

Saunders, Graham. *About Kane: The Playwright and the Work*. London: Faber and Faber, 2009.

Saunders, Graham. " 'If There Could Have Been More Moments like This': Phaedra's Love." In *Sarah Kane in Context*, 71–81. Manchester: Manchester University Press, 2010.

Sierz, Aleks. *In-Yer-Face Theatre: British Drama Today*. London: Faber and Faber, 2001.

Sierz, Aleks. Rev. of Phaedra"s Love, by Sarah Kane, Dir. Kane, The Gate Theatre, Notting Hill, *Tribune*, 20 May-15 June 1996.

Vangölü, Yeliz Biber. "Sarah Kane's *Cleansed* as a Critical Assessment of Disciplinary Power." *Ankara University The Journal of the Faculty of Languages and History-Geography*, 57, no. 1 (2017): 274–288.

Wallace, Clare. "Sarah Kane, experiential theatre and the revenant avant-garde." In *Sarah Kane in Context*, edited by L. de Vos and G. Saunders, 88–99. Manchester and New York: Manchester University Press, 2010.

Ward, Ian. "Rape and Rape Mythology in the Plays of Sarah Kane." *Comparative Drama*, 47, no. 2 (2013): 225–248.

Enes Kavak and Gökçe Akarık

Nostalgia and Identity Crisis of Black British Characters in Roy Williams's *The No Boys Cricket Club*

Introduction

Roy Williams (1968–) is a successful representative of contemporary Black British theatre, which has mainly dealt with racial and social issues of modern English society. As the author of the award-winning *Sucker Punch*, he earned his initial reputation with *The No Boys Cricket Club* in 1996. The play was a bold experiment, but it proved to be a success by bringing him the Writer's Guild New Writer of the Year award in 1996.[1] Williams's early trilogy, which includes *The No Boys Cricket Club* (1996), *Starstruck* (1997) and *The Gift* (2000), draws on his own life and depicts the experiences and domestic troubles of the first-generation Jamaicans in Britain. While the plays mainly focus on the characters' struggle between their Jamaican heritage and their British identity, his later plays look into contemporary culture by presenting "the experiences of [second generation of] Jamaican emigrants in Britain through the stories on "the 'painful' experiences of a young, urban, Black population, dealing with violence, racism within the law, gang conflict and sexual politics."[2] The young Black characters in these plays epitomize young members of the Anglo-Caribbean community who have been born in England and found themselves in a current of shifting politics, socio-economic difficulties and individual problems. By appropriating his first-hand knowledge of the diaspora, the playwright has encouraged his readers and audiences to question the dynamics of a multicultural society they live in by

1 Alex Sierz notes that *The No Boys Cricket Club* featured a large cast and the play was a product of the writer's school years at Rose Bruford College in Kent. For further details, see Alex Sierz, "Playwright Roy Williams: The prolific playwright talks about football and racism," 24 October 2009, Theartsdesk.com. https://theartsdesk.com/theatre/theartsdesk-qa-playwright-roy-williams? page=0%2C1.

2 Elizabeth Barry and William Boles, "Beyond Victimhood: Agency and Identity in the Theatre of Roy Williams," in Alternatives within the Mainstream British Black and Asian Theatres, edited by Dimple Godiwala (Newcastle: Cambridge Scholars Press, 2006), 297–312.

barraging them with stories of nostalgia, identity crisis, family feud and racial discrimination.

The No Boys Cricket Club narrates two Jamaican women's search for identity outside the spatio-temporal reality of their new lives in East London. Williams disclosed that the lead character is "a middle-aged woman called Abigail, whom [he] loosely based on [his] mother."[3] Reflecting upon his personal experiences, he manages to construct convincing Black characters to show the contradictions and dilemmas of urban multiculturalism in British society. The play is particularly notable with the nostalgia-driven, first-generation Jamaican characters and this chapter aims to explore the characters' spatio-temporal identity quest triggered by nostalgia and constant pursuit of belonging.

The Construction of Nostalgia and Black British Identity in *The No Boys Cricket Club*

Although it was widely written on the works of Black American writers in the second half of the twentieth century, the plays of Black British playwrights had not received the same amount of academic interest until the 2000s.[4] Lynette Goddard states, "the first decade of the twenty-first century saw a perceivable shift in the fortunes of Black British playwrights who started to gain a more high-profile mainstream presence than they had achieved before."[5] These playwrights revealed the social and cultural problems that they and their contemporaries experience regularly in their daily lives and wrote more on the topics that had been side-lined and overlooked by directors, critics and middle-class theatre-goers in the 70s and 80s. Daniela Salusso describes this new period's theatre as "a kind of theatre which distances itself both from the postcolonial tradition and from the generation of the in-yer-face theatre and attempts rather to redefine

3 Roy Williams, "Roy Williams, in conversation with Aleks Sierz What Kind of England Do We Want?" New Theatre Quarterly 22, no. 2 (2006): 115.

4 To illustrate, Errol Hill offers very detailed examinations of Black American Theatre in the 1980s with a series of critical essays in Errol Hill, The Theater of Black Americans (Englewood Cliffs, NJ: Prentice-Hall, 1980). Studies on Black British Theatre appeared mostly after the 2000s as Black playwrights such as Kwame Kwei-Armah, debbie tucker green, Roy Williams and Bola Agbaje wrote plays on Black people's experiences in the last two decades.

5 Lynette Goddard, Contemporary Black British Playwrights: Margins to Mainstream (London: Palgrave Macmillan, 2015), 4.

British identity through a 'hybridisation' of the theatrical discourse."[6] The studies have shown that they depart from the conventions and style of the first-generation émigré writers and they become much more visible and productive in the mainstream theatres.

Denoting hybridity, plurality and transnationality, "Black British" is a broad concept encompassing the majority of immigrants that have settled in the British Isles. These diverse groups of people have different personality traits, linguistic backgrounds and cultural values. Tracy J. Prince notes that

> The term Black British gained currency in the mid-1970s and was used primarily as a political signifier. Within the British context, the word "Black" has been used to refer to African, Caribbean and South Asian settlers. In Britain, the umbrella term Black British facilitated a political alliance across second generation immigrants from very different cultures who came together to organise collectively against their common experiences of institutional and individual racism.[7]

This transnational designation is a product of historical, political and economic factors that are ingrained in the colonial history of Britain, which produced a large body of literature portraying cross-cultural and cross-national representations and interactions by expanding the boundaries of the concept of "home." Bronwyn T. Williams points out, "being identified as "British" is an important public and overtly political act, in fact [Black British writers'] work continues to emphasize the catachrestic nature of the term, how it lacks a true referent in a transnational, diasporic world."[8] Black British identity can thus be associated with fluidity, belonging and transnational/cultural interaction. Literature on the topic has often portrayed Black characters' dilemmas over maintaining their identity and their inner conflicts resulting from the feelings of loss and failure. The tension and anxiety of these constant struggles offer a fertile ground for the portrayals of nostalgia and identity crisis.

---

6 Daniela Salusso, ""The "Diasporic Theatre" from Nostalgia to Contemporary Sociopolitics: Reimagining Identity in Some Contemporary Black and Asian British Playwrights," Il castello di Elsinore 66, (2020): 67–76.

7 Tracy J. Prince, "Black British," in Companion to Contemporary Black British Culture, edited by Allison Donnell (London: Routledge, 2002), 40–41.

8 Bronwyn T. Williams, "A State of Perpetual Wandering: Diaspora and Black British Writers." *Jouvert: A Journal of Postcolonial Studies* 3, no. 3 (1999): 38. https://legacy.chass.ncsu.edu/jouvert/v3i3/willia.htm

Nostalgia originates etymologically from "nostos" in Greek, which means "returning to home" and "algos," standing for "suffering" or "grief"[9] and it features both positive and negative emotions. From a temporal perspective, it signifies the past life and experiences and can refer to the reminiscences of pleasant and unpleasant times in someone's life. This goes beyond the historical meaning of nostalgia as "homesickness" in the modern world. Davis (1979) defines nostalgia as a phenomenon permitting individuals to preserve their identity during transitory periods, complications and disruptions.[10] Past experiences, memories and life-changing events, most of which are subjective and unique for each individual can evoke nostalgia-driven spurs and trigger nostalgic and melancholic intervals. At this point, nostalgia should be distinguished from an often-mixed concept of melancholy. Similar to melancholy, "acute nostalgia was activated and exacerbated by an unhappy consciousness of self, in this case, a self that was embedded in memories of home."[11] Freud asserts that melancholia "remains sunken in his loss, unable to acknowledge and accept the need to cleave and in a self-destructive loyalty to the lost object, internalizes it into his ego, thus furthermore circumscribing the conflict related to the loss."[12] Mathew Bell argues that melancholia can be understood better as a culture-bound syndrome[13] and he maintains that historically "melancholia has been an experience of people in the West more or less consistently since antiquity. … melancholia is dependent on a peculiar feature of Western culture – namely, the exceptionally high value that Western culture assigns to inwardness and self-consciousness."[14] Nostalgia, yet, refers to a personal life experience and the recollections of events and past that have not been lived by a certain person that can have the potential to create nostalgic emotions.[15] Nostalgia is thus more associated with a bitter-sweet sentimentality

9 Eugene B. Daniels, "Nostalgia and Hidden Meaning," American Imago 42, no. 4 (1985): 371.

10 Fred Davis, Yearning for *Yesterday*: A Sociology of Nostalgia (New York: Free Press, 1979).

11 Matthew Bell, Melancholia: The Western Malady (Cambridge: Cambridge University Press, 2014), 112.

12 Ilit Ferber, "Melancholy Philosophy: Freud and Benjamin," *E-rea. Revue électronique d'études sur le monde anglophone* 4.1 (2006): 1. DOI: https://doi.org/10.4000/erea.413

13 Bell, *Melancholia*, 115.

14 Ibid.

15 William J. Havlena and Susan L. Holak, "'The Good Old Days'; Observations on Nostalgia and İts Role in Consumer Behavior," *ACR North American Advances* (1991): 323–329.

about the past and loss of "home" or a sense of belonging while melancholy is much more about one's state of gloom, depression or sadness without a necessary connection with the past or any loss. In the light of this delineation, the rest of this chapter will examine the subjective quality of nostalgia through two major characters from Black Caribbean heritage, Abigail (Abi) and Masie, who travel beyond the temporal limits of the present in the reclamation of their past in *No Boys Cricket Club*.[16]

The play oscillates between two places, Kingston, Jamaica and East London, which reveals the dilemmas and disappointments of two Black female characters in their domestic lives. The central character, Abi (53), is a widow whose son, Michael, is a drug dealer and daughter, Danielle is harassed by gangs of other girls in the community. Abi is stuck between her past in Jamaica and her role as a homemaker of a disintegrating family. Her childhood friend, Masie, whose son was killed by White mobs and whose marriage crackles, takes Abi to the childhood times in Jamaica when they were members of a female-only cricket club. In a postmodern twist, Maise insists that Abi should attempt to rewrite their own stories by giving their young selves advice about their choices and deconstruct their lives as high-achieving young girls. Abi communicates with her younger and ambitious Jamaican self and opens up her feeling about her hopes and challenging family relations. This is the only connection between her and Jamaica, which represents an imaginary escape to heal and come to terms with her anguish and disenchantment. Although she is frightened of what she is doing at first, she achieves to go deeper to solve her inner troubles. Her initial strife and later introspection reveal that she is trapped in the happy memories of her childhood, which she cannot manage to revive in her unhappy adulthood. The *raisons d'être* of a play featuring a character like Abi is explained by Williams as follows:

> It was staged in 1996, two years before the celebration of the Windrush generation – named after the first boat that left the West Indies to come to England in 1948. … And one day I just asked her, "Why don't you go back to Jamaica?" and she said, "No, I don't want to do that, I want to stay here." And I said, "When you talk about it your face lights up," and she said, "Well that's the past, that's what it is, the past." And, years ago, she did actually go home and she said, "That's not the Jamaica I know, it's more troubled now, very violent now." So I incorporated that into the play as well. It's about belonging, which

16 Roy Williams, Plays I (London: Methuen Drama, 2002). This edition will be used for further references to the primary text, which will hereafter be cited as in "*The No Boys Cricket Club*, page no."

seems to be a common theme in all my plays, a central character who's lost, looking for that sense of belonging.[17]

Williams constructs the story on two familiar issues: generation gap and immigrants' mental/material resistance against the change. As the writer reveals, Abi's nostalgia is a silent articulation of longing for self-expression. Her self-blame after the death of her unloving mother is resolved when she accepts to change herself and her social milieu. To embody the tension in the Black community, the play depends on several binary oppositions shaping the lives of two female characters such as fantasy/real, ordinary/exceptional, past/present, Jamaican/British and the young/the old. Particularly, the daydream scenes of the play show the desire of Black female characters to break away from spatio-temporal realities to take refuge in an imaginative territory. On the one hand, the daydreams take Masie and Abi back to Jamaica in romantic and nostalgic time-travel; on the other hand, a life laden with violence, poverty and shattered relationships constitute the authenticity of migrants' life in the suburbs of East London. Scott Alexander Howard emphasizes "nostalgia involves a judgment that the past was better."[18] He defines this as "the poverty of the present requirement,"[19] which suggests "the intentional object of nostalgia is necessarily a past regarded as preferable to the present."[20] That is, nostalgia is a strong desire to return to one's previous happy life as a way to evade the burden of the present. Aside from its temporal nature, "nostalgia" has a spatial aspect, as it "is literally the suffering due to a relentless yearning for the homeland."[21] The old Abi's conversation with the young self about how she felt disappointed and alienated as a child when her family moved from the country to Kingston, Jamaica reveals such a sentiment:

Masie and I spent ages visiting our old haunts, that sorta thing. All the way down Lambert Street we went: we saw Miss Stuart still sitting on her stool on the corner, *(laughs)* the Brewster boys, Masie's house, my house. It hadn't changed a bit, every door, every window looked exactly the same. I never liked that place you know, it was her house, Miss Tyler's! Staring at it made me remember the day we first moved there. I was seven and we left the country to live in Kingston, and I remember seeing this little

17 Williams, "Roy Williams, in conversation with Aleks Sierz," 115.

18 Scott Alexander Howard. "Nostalgia," *Analysis* 72, no. 4 (2012): 643.

19 Ibid.

20 Ibid.

21 Constantine Sedikides, Tim Wildschut, Jamie Arndt, and Clay Routledge. "Nostalgia: Past, Present, and Future," Current Directions in Psychological Science 17, no. 5 (2008): 304.

> summing of a house perched on this hill [...] Oh, sweet Jamaica. *(Puts her arms around herself, giving herself a cuddle).* Masie was right. I feel, reunited wid my soul. *(Laughs.)* 'Hello soul, hello Abi. Long time no hear girl!' Long time.[22]

Masie asks Abi "when was the last time you really thought about home?"[23] and at Masie's insistence, Abi reluctantly consents to her proposal to reform her unfulfilled life. Her attachment to Jamaica prompts a nostalgic image of her youth as a source of hope and aspiration, so the past turns into a more preferable setting than the present can offer. Oliveira notes that Jamaica "leads to the feeling of displacement in the place where the characters migrated to. It is so because it is the place where they were happy and they felt secure."[24] Daydreaming appears to be both a getaway and a creative space for them to deconstruct the narratives of the "Windrush generation."[25] When the first time Abi and Masie daydream, Abi cannot distinguish whether it is real or not, Masie responds to her as "we wished, it happened, who cares about the in-between? Not me darling."[26] As Davis's states, this "third order of nostalgia" offers them a new realm for understanding the nostalgic experience itself.[27] Since she does not have the opportunity to evade familial responsibilities, the daydreams become a substitute, a fictional life in which she can keep her memories alive and belong somewhere. This journey thus turns into a metaphor for separation and reunion between Abi and her younger self, past and present, and repressed emotions and their articulation.

22 *The No Boys Cricket Club*, 55.

23 Ibid., 29.

24 Célia Maria Silva Oliveira, "From the Margins into the Mainstream: Roy Williams and Black British Theatre (1995–2010)." Thesis, Universidade do Minho, 2012, 33.

25 The Caribbean people who immigrated to Britain between 1948 and 1971 have often been labelled as the "Windrush generation," which is a reference to the ship MV Empire Windrush, which brought workers in 1948 to solve labour shortages in Britain after the the Second World War. For a more detailed discussion, see "Windrush generation: Who are they and why are they facing problems?" 31 July 2020, *BBC News*. https://www.bbc.com/news/uk-43782241

26 *The No Boys Cricket Club*, 32.

27 Susan L. Holak and William J. Havlena note "Davis distinguishes among three levels of nostalgic experience. First order or simple nostalgia is associated with the simple, unquestioning belief that "things were better in the past." Second order or reflexive nostalgia involves a critical analysis of the past rather than sentimentalization of it. Finally, in third order or interpreted nostalgia, the individual analyzes the nostalgic experience itself" (Susan L. Holak and William J. Havlena, "Nostalgia: An Exploratory Study of Themes and Emotions in the Nostalgic Experience," *NA – Advances in Consumer Research*, 19 (1992): 380–387).

Roy Williams portrays Abi as a woman in constant dilemma and impasse. Abi's son, Michael, blames her for not being an ideal mother due to her obsession with loss and regret. He says "wat am I talkin' to you for? You don't know how to. You're nuttin without Dad. All you do is go on about sweet Jamaica."[28] As Abi fails to grow up and build a proper connection with her children after the death of her mother and husband, her spatial existence in London alienates her as a Black woman, a mother of upset children and a non-functioning member of the society. Her separation from Jamaica is the very reason for her angst and existential crises preventing her from assuming a meaningful identity in the present. This state of Abi can be understood better with the critical concept of "place attachment." The concept has been widely used by theorists with various phrasings such as

> "community attachment" by Kasarda and Janowitz in 1974, "sense of community" by Sarason in 1974, "place attachment" by Gerson et al. in 1977, "place identity" by Proshansky in 1978, "place dependence" by Stokols and Shumaker in 1981 and "sense of place" in Hummon in 1992.[29]

Place attachment can be outlined "as an affective bond or link between people and specific places."[30] Low and Altman note "places are repositories and contexts within which interpersonal, community and cultural relationships occur, and it is to those social relationships, not just to place qua place, to which people are attached."[31] Williams uses Jamaica as a fictional setting for Abi and many Caribbean immigrants to attach to and culturally identify with, as they are part of a community in which they share the same cultural values and engage in meaningful interactions. However, Britain is portrayed with personal, social and economic troubles, so they have to go through the mental process of gaining a new identity and achieving a painful detachment. The oscillation between these two worlds generates a world of theatrical and cultural embodiment and transformation on stage outside the temporal authenticity of life. Williams uses this transformative quality of theatre with the metaphorical power of events and objects. Havlena and Holak point out that events and memories evoking later nostalgic spurs are mostly leisure activities, that the subject and peers build a sense of membership and belonging among its partakers.[32] In the play, the world of the past is linked by a play of cricket, a metaphor for a romantic connection with youth and the

---

28 *The No Boys Cricket Club*, 52.

29 M. Carmen Hidalgo and Bernardo Hernandez. "Place Attachment: Conceptual and Empirical Questions." Journal of *Environmental Psychology* 21, no. 3 (2001): 273.

30 Ibid., 274

31 Cited in Hidalgo and Hernandez, "Place Attachment," 275.

32 Havlena and Holak, "Nostalgia," 323–329.

mature self. It is in this theatrical realm that the two Abi help each other to take on the half-completed life and settle down their story. Cricket also symbolizes Abi's success in a teenage all-girls cricket team in Jamaica, where she can compete with the boys' team for gender equality. In this sense, cricket is not only a cultural engagement but also a potential vehicle for female progress and public recognition in a male-dominated society.

Masie is another disenchanted woman living in the Black British diaspora. Her son, Jeffrey becomes the victim of a brutal racial crime committed by a White gang. This trauma makes the already problematic life of Masie more excruciating and turns into a catalyst for her fantasy-driven escapism. Her quarrel with her husband Ferdy, on his inciting furry and hatred to Jeffrey, reveals two sides of a coin: the impasse of the Black British diaspora in the face of exacerbating incidents of racial discrimination and growing Black nationalism. Ferdy admits that he does not feel regret about what his son has done: "I'm proud of what he did! […] it's our war, we fight it ourselves."[33] He holds the view that Black diaspora have only one chance to defend their rights through violence and he feels proud of his son's dignified resistance. Alison Donnell declares that "the political and ideological struggle over 'blackness' continues,"[34] and there is a long way for complete equality even in today's multicultural societies. As Frantz Fanon claims, the Black diaspora shows the reaction in the same way White does, and this leads to dreadful experiences for the Black diaspora in return.[35] In the case of Jeffrey, the Black diaspora represents the failure of hybrid lives they have to maintain due to physical violence along with its psychological effects. He asks "How accepted are we? On the surface it's changed; we don't have signs saying 'No blacks, no Irish, no dogs.' […] But what I'm asking in my plays, is: have they really? Is it just all on the surface? Are we really as safe and well as we say we are?"[36] The members of the diaspora still endure the incidents of hate crimes putting them in a symbolic exile, "a psychological, philosophical, and existential condition that defines this experience of migration as displacement, loss, and homelessness."[37]

33 *The No Boys Cricket Club*, 48.

34 Prince, "Black British." 41.

35 Frantz Fanon, *Black Skin, White Masks*. Translated by Charles Lam Markmann (London: Pluto Press, 1968).

36 *The No Boys Cricket Club*, 116.

37 Yana Meerzon, "On the Paradigms of Banishment, Displacement, and Free Choice," in Performing Exile: Foreign Bodies, edited by Judith Rudakoff (Bristol: Intellect, 2017), 17–36, 19.

Apart from Williams's political message on the need for further discussion on racial discrimination and violence through Jeffrey's murder, he creates a "third space" in the play, a hybrid of real and fantastic layers of the story representing the liminal identities Black immigrants maintain in various disguises. The concept of hybridity is the key to the construction of Black identity in the writer's plays on multicultural England. The in-betweenness of characters with their Anglo-Jamaican identities destabilizes the binary oppositions and established norms of the host culture. A theoretical explanation of this hybridity can be made by the concept of "thirdspace," which was coined by the geographer, Edward William Soja, to attribute to the "thirding" processes of modern multicultural city life. According to Soja, thirdspace emerges as a result of the process of "thirding-as-Othering': a voice simultaneously from the margins and the center, the future and the past, the infinite possibilities of space from all points and times simultaneously."[38] The co-existence of multiple temporal and spatial presence creates a potent space for creativity and subversion. The thirdspace, in this way, "challenges our sense of historical identity of culture as a homogenizing, unifying force [… and] constitutes the discursive conditions of enunciation that ensure the meaning and symbols of culture have no primordial unity or fixity."[39] That is, thirdspace defies fixation, labels and stereotypes because there is no heterogeneous historicity of identities and cultures in this time-space.

Owing to the mutual interaction of the West and East, culture in "thirdspace" is vulnerable to deconstruction and transformation with the integration of different racial-ethnic groups, creating a transnational and/or transcultural atmosphere. Multi-ethnic East London stands as a good example for thirdspace. Even though Masie rejects caring about being in-between in a liminal existence, she reveals the difficulty of feeling stuck in such a state. The separation from the homeland has a propounding effect on Masie as well as Abi, who states her disappointment in her conversation with the younger Abi: "but I've never bin the same since I came to England. Day by day everything just went out of me."[40] The words of the women point up to an existential crisis arising from being "in-between." The interaction of a human being with the environment is the basic criteria for having a sense of the world in which the human relations are set, and for Massie, "place is space to which the meaning has been ascribed."[41]

38 Stuart Aitken, "Thirdspace: Journeys to Los Angeles and Other Real-and-Imagined Places by Edward W. Soja,." *Geographical Review* 88, no. 1 (1998): 149.

39 Homi K. Bhabha, The Location of Culture (London: Routledge, 1994), 37.

40 *The No Boys Cricket Club*, 62.

41 Carter et al., 1993, p. xii, cited in Doreen Massey, For space (London: SAGE, 2005), 183.

The sense of belonging to a place occupies an important position in making sense of life since place and being are interconnected. The memories lived in a specific place constitute the whole meaning of experiences and thus these memories play a significant role to attach one to that specific place. As Altman and Low emphasize that "place attachment may contribute to the formation, maintenance, and preservation of the identity of a person, group, or culture."[42] Masie is stuck in between two opposite places and this is a source of her suffering. Setting a purpose and creating meaning for life is thus actualized in the border of that attached place. For this reason, a nostalgic "topophilia"[43] is observed in the minority communities and diasporas as a consequence of failure in identification with and attachment to the host culture. Jamaican characters in the play reveal such a reality about immigration and integration. In the multi-ethnic and multicultural world, mixed racial and liminal groups are supposed to lead their lives in search of equality, agreeable economic standards and political rights as the White majority. Their in-between statuses challenge and undermine the boundaries of the power of the new society, and prompt them to resist coercion and stereotypification.

Conclusion

Daniela Salusso asserts that "diasporic theatre challenges our notions of nation and identity at their very roots … What is unique in this generation of diasporic writers is the condition of duality and the hybrid position from which they write."[44] Black characters in these plays represent Black people from different classes, settings, and political views portrayed in transnational and transgenerational interactions within their inner circles as well as with the White majority. Contemporary Black writers thus turn their liminal dramatic stages as a metaphor for the liminal Black lives. Together with other contemporary Black British playwrights, Roy Williams's theatre holds up a unique mirror to the British society about ordinary people's struggle with multinationalism, cultural integration and rising urban youth.

The No Boys Cricket Club, in this respect, draws on Williams's life and his relationship with his mother as a model for Abi, who is a Jamaican migrant in

---

42 Altman and Low, 5.

43 "Topophilia" is defined as "human love of a place" in Yi-Fu Tuan, *Topophilia: a Study of Environmental Perception, Attitudes, and Values. New York* (Colombia University Press, 1974), 92.

44 Salusso, "The 'Diasporic Theatre,'" 68.

England. The play offers an early example of the playwright's wish to stage Black lives and their problems in the mainstream. Therefore, Abi and Maisie's disenchantment represents the first-generation Caribbean migrants' family issues and existential worries about their future. This common theme was not new to the play as the 1980s and 1990s experienced a surge of such plays concentrating on the first-generation immigrants. However, as R. Victoria Arana and Lauri Ramey put it, "the neo-millennial avant-garde artists are clear about wishing to distinguish their voices from those of the preceding ("postcolonial") generation and very explicit about differentiating their neo-millennial aspirations from the old (colonialist and imperialist) ethos of Great Britain."[45] Williams's early plays offer a mixture of personal issues and contemporary social problems troubling the Caribbean community in England. As a part of this strategy, the play narrates an imaginative quest instigated by nostalgia and existential anxieties of characters, for whom the past is imagined as a liminal space for reclamation and transformation of the future. Setting the scenes in both Britain and Jamaica, Williams employs fantastic elements in the play and expresses the immigrants' desire to destabilize the public narratives of suffering and healing. Accordingly, Williams relies on the transformative power of theatre and attempts to reach the general public with the offer of a unique theatrical experience and creative social criticism.

Bibliography

Aitken, Stuart. "Thirdspace: Journeys to Los Angeles and Other Real-and-Imagined Places by Edward W. Soja." *Geographical Review* 88, no. 1 (1998): 148–151. https://doi.org/10.2307/215881.

Altman, Irwin, and Setha M. Low, eds. "Place Attachment: A Conceptual Inquiry," in *Place Attachment*, 1–12, New York: Plenum Press, 1992.

Arana, R. Victoria, and Lauri Ramey, eds. *Black British Writing*. New York: Palgrave Macmillan, 2004.

Barry, Elizabeth, and William Boles, "Beyond Victimhood: Agency and Identity in the Theatre of Roy Williams," in *Alternatives Within the Mainstream British Black and Asian Theatres*, edited by Dimple Godiwala, 297–312, Newcastle: Cambridge Scholars Press, 2006.

Bell, Matthew, *Melancholia: The Western Malady*,. Cambridge: Cambridge University Press, 2014.

45 R. Victoria Arana and Lauri Ramey, eds. *Black British Writing* (New York: Palgrave Macmillan, 2004), 2.

Bhabha, Homi K, *The Location of Culture*. London: Routledge, 1994.

Daniels, Eugene B. "Nostalgia and Hidden Meaning." *American Imago* 42, no. 4 (1985): 371–383.

Davis, Fred. *Yearning for Yesterday: A Sociology of Nostalgia*. New York: Free Press, 1979.

Fanon, Frantz. *Black Skin, White Masks*. Trans. Charles Lam Markmann. London: Pluto Press, 1968.

Ferber, Ilit. "Melancholy Philosophy: Freud and Benjamin." *E-rea. Revue électronique d'études sur le monde anglophone* 4.1 (2006). DOI: https://doi.org/10.4000/erea.413

Goddard, Lynette. *Contemporary Black British Playwrights: Margins to Mainstream*. London: Palgrave Macmillan, 2015.

Hidalgo, M. Carmen, and Bernardo Hernandez. "Place Attachment: Conceptual and Empirical Questions," *Journal of Environmental Psychology* 21, no. 3 (2001): 273–281.

Hill, Errol. *The Theater of Black Americans*. Englewood Cliffs, NJ: Prentice-Hall, 1980.

Havlena, William J. and Susan L. Holak. " 'The Good Old Day': Observations on Nostalgia and Its Role in Consumer Behavior," *ACR North American Advances*, no. 18 (1991): 323–329.

Holak, Susan L. and William J. Havlena, "Nostalgia: an Exploratory Study of Themes andEmotions in the Nostalgic Experience," *NA - Advances in Consumer Research*, 19 (1992): 380–387.

Howard, Scott Alexander. "Nostalgia," *Analysis* 72, no. 4 (2012): 641–650. https://doi.org/10.1093/analys/ans105.

Massey, Doreen. *For Space*. London: Sage, 2005.

Meerzon, Yana. "On the Paradigms of Banishment, Displacement, and Free Choice," in *Performing Exile: Foreign Bodies*, edited by Judith Rudakoff, 17–36, Bristol: Intellect, 2017.

Oliveira, Célia Maria Silva. "From the Margins into the Mainstream: Roy Williams and Black British Theatre (1995–2010)." Thesis, Universidade do Minho, 2012.

Prince, Tracy J., "Black British," in *Companion to Contemporary Black British Culture*, edited by Allison Donnell, 40–41, London: Routledge, 2013.

Sedikides, Constantine, Tim Wildschut, Jamie Arndt, and Clay Routledge. "Nostalgia: Past, Present, and Future," *Current Directions in Psychological Science* 17, no. 5 (2008): 304–307.

Salusso, Daniela. "The "Diasporic Theatre" from Nostalgia to Contemporary Socio-politics: Reimagining Identity in Some Contemporary Black and Asian British Playwrights," *Il castello di Elsinore* 66 (2012): 67–76.

Sierz, Alex. "Playwright Roy Williams: The Prolific Playwright Talks about Football and Racism," 24 October 2009, Theartsdesk.com. https://theartsdesk.com/theatre/theartsdesk-qa-playwright-roy-williams?page=0%2C1.

Williams, Bronwyn T. "A State of Perpetual Wandering: Diaspora and Black British Writers," Jouvert: *A Journal of Postcolonial Studies* 3, no. 3 (1999): 38. https://legacy.chass.ncsu.edu/jouvert/v3i3/willia.htm

Williams, Roy. *Plays I*. London: Methuen Drama, 2002.

Williams, Roy. "Roy Williams, in Conversation with Aleks Sierz: What Kind of England Do We Want?" *New Theatre Quarterly* 22, no. 2 (2006): 113–121.

"Windrush Generation: Who Are They and Why Are They Facing Problems?" 31 July 2020, BBC News. https://www.bbc.com/news/uk-43782241.

Mustafa Bal

Apocalypse In-Yer-Face: Mark Ravenhill's *Faust Is Dead*[1]

Introduction

The conceptualization of decades in history is a demonstration of *endist* or apocalyptic discourse[2]: each decade begins and ends in a period of ten years, and each harbours a peculiar character. We call them the 50s, 60s, 70s, 80s and so on. The 1990s was a decade of personal computers, the internet, mobile phones, digital cameras, genocides, economic productivity, capitalism, globalization, AIDS, the fall of the Berlin wall and the end of the Cold War with the collapse of the Soviet Union, the fall of Margaret Thatcher, the Gulf War, Generation X, developments in DNA technology and cloning, digital games, tattooing and body-piercing, expanded freedom and outspokenness of the culture of homosexuality, TV reality shows, extreme sports, hip-hop, techno and underground music, alternative rock and the scandalous death of Lady Diana. It was also an apocalyptic age as the ideas of the end were intensified and revealed through these closing years of the second millennium. So was it for the British drama which, through the In-Yer-Face sensibility, produced an attempt to shape-shift projections of reality on the stage. In its idiosyncrasies for changing representations of reality, there was an underlying tone of *endism* or apocalypticism in the 1990s playwriting aesthetics. Considering these, this study investigates how and to what extent the In-Yere-Face playwright Mark Ravenhill makes use of the apocalyptic discourse in his play *Faust Is Dead*, and argues that the apocalyptic rhetoric in the play emerges through a set of philosophical ideas and theories by thinkers such as (and primarily) Michel Foucault and Jean Baudrillard.

Faust Is Dead had its debut in 1997, a year after *Shopping and F***ing* introduced Mark Ravenhill and secured him a career as a promising playwright. Ravenhill's story of the writing of the play owes much to the first director of the play, Nick Philippou, who, as he reveals in his interview with Enric Monforte,

1 This study is culled from the author's unpublished PhD dissertation, entitled "The End: The Apocalyptic in In-Yer-Face Drama," Middle East Technical University, 2009.

2 In this study, terms *apocalypse* and *the end* (or their derivatives) will be used interchangeably.

urged him to write "a contemporary Faust to be based on the life of Michel Foucault."[3] However, as Ravenhill continued searching, he "came to Jean Baudrillard, whom I found a more resonant writer than Foucault."[4] In this sense, the play makes use of several of the most influential apocalyptic theories of the twentieth century like Foucauldian end of History, the death of Man, and the change of the order of the subject and object due to technological advances and progress in mass production; and Baudrillardian end of reality and the beginning of a virtual world of the simulacra of hyperreality. The play blended these theories with a remaking of the classical Faust myth, which Aleks Sierz, likewise, observes when he writes, "Using his characteristic mix of postmodern ideas and traditional morality, Ravenhill's *Faust is Dead* is a good example of the decade's freedom in turning old myths into new sources of meaning."[5]

Apocalyptic Discourse in *Faust Is Dead*

It is not misleading to say that the play's apocalypticism starts with its title. The idea of the end of life is initiated with the word "dead" in the title. The title sounds doubly apocalyptic as it trumpets the end of one of the most well-known stories, and of its representative character, Faust. The story of the legendary tale of Faust, a man who makes a pact with Satan to obtain the highest level of knowledge in return for his promise of allegiance to devil, has been used many times in literature and art,[6] and Ravenhill's play brings out the legend more apocalyptically than ever in having its title announce the demise of the archetypal character. In this sense, the title points to a cultural loss as well.

"Who represents Faust in the play" is a question which needs an answer in relation to the title. Is it Pete or Alain? Pete appears as a character standing in for the legendary character as, paralleling the story of Faust, he holds the power of knowledge in the format of software, which allows him to approach the

3 Mark Ravenhill, "Mark Ravenhill," interview by Enric Monforte, *British Theatre of the 1990s: Interviews with Directors, Playwrights, Critics and Academics*, edited by Mireia Aragay, Hildegard Klein, Enric Monforte, and Pilar Zozoya (New York: Palgrave Macmillan, 2007), 96.

4 Ibid., 96.

5 Aleks Sierz, In-Yer-Face Theatre: British Drama Today (London: Faber and Faber, 2000), 138.

6 Among the works based on Faust, Christopher Marlowe's play *The Tragical History of Doctor Faustus*, Johann Wolfgang von Goethe's *Faust*, and Thomas Mann's *Doktor Faustus* are well-known works.

position of a "God, God, God"[7] in each house. He is planning to sell the disc for a huge sum of money, with which he is planning to "buy so many totally real experiences,"[8] which, again echoing Faust's conjured experiences all over the world, gives him the possibility of indulging in action and relations on a world scale: "I'm gonna keep the peace in Bosnia. I'm gonna take Saddam Hussein out for a pizza. I'm gonna shoot pool with the Pope and have Boris Yeltsin show me his collection of baseball stickers."[9] All his fantasies seem to involve mockery of world leaders, one more time recalling Doctor Faustus' travels and relations to world leaders like the Pope, and the German Emperor Charles V. In pursuing such power, Pete poses as the Faust of the play. However, Alain will prove to be a better Faust than Pete as the play progresses. Alain does not represent Faust as a man of action and trickeries (unlike Pete) but is rather the philosophical Faust. If the play shows the death of Faust, then it matches Alain's death at the end of the play, which is also the death of man "as an idea, as a construct."[10] Beeping sounds, each time "louder and shriller"[11] in the hospital scene at the end of the play, correspond to the strikes of the clock at the end of Marlowe's *Doctor Faustus*; no less, Donny, coming from the abode of the dead, may be matching Mephistopheles or the devils who come to carry Doctor Faustus to hell at the end of Marlowe's play. Alain also represents the twentieth century knowledgeable man, and dies, marking the death of well-informed man whose archetype is found in the Faust myth. As is obvious, both Pete and Alain carry Faustian features, showing that Ravenhill does not recreate an exact replica of the Faust in his play. His is rather a postmodern re-characterization of the figure. Instead of the meta-narrative of Faust, Ravenhill presents Fausts. Similarly, Aleks Sierz observes Alain as Faust and comes to the following conclusion: "Ravenhill's Alain keeps changing places, one moment being Faust, the next Mephistopheles, which not only underlines the idea that good and evil coexist, but also dramatizes postmodern ideas about the volatility of character and the indeterminacy of the subject."[12]

The apocalypticism of *Faust Is Dead* carries a strong sense of crisis. Crisis embraces the play from top to toe. As the play opens, a worldwide crisis is introduced with the speech of Chorus:

7 Mark Ravenhill, *Plays 1: Shopping and F***ing, Faust Is Dead, Handbag, Some Explicit Polaroids* (London: Methuen Drama, 2001), 111.

8 Ravenhill, *Plays 1*, 112.

9 Ibid., 112.

10 Ibid., 98.

11 Ibid., 139.

12 Sierz, *In-Yer-Face Theatre*, 136.

> CHORUS: See, a few years ago I couldn't sleep. I'd go to bed and then I got thinking about all this stuff in the world – about the riots and the fighting and all the angry people and all – and I just couldn't sleep. And sometimes I'd cry – partly because I really wanted to sleep and I was mad that I couldn't sleep but partly because of all those bad things going on.[13]

Chorus would cry and his mother would then come to sooth him, yet he would cry "for the world, because the world is such a bad place."[14] With this opening speech of the play, Chorus, which, in harmony with its classical roots, is supposed to represent the community, imposes a heavily critical tone to the play: the world is a bad place and life is unpleasant. More, the predicament of the world is an immediate one, lived here and now, as the setting suggests that it is "present day,"[15] rather than a narration of a past emergency. With the crisis appealing to the moment, the apocalyptic mood is prepared as apocalyptic anxieties flourish during times of crises.

The immediacy of crisis is strengthened with the fact of the growing digitalization of the world. One example of this is found in scene thirteen where Chorus recounts one of his childhood memories, in which a church father leads a charity campaign to raise funds to buy computer terminals for the church, hoping that "young people" will be "online" inside the church and will spread religious doctrines from there.[16] Nevertheless, the expectations of the church father and mothers, who worked very hard to accomplish the project are not met, as the response of the children is to become addicted to the internet and spend all their time with it. The church father interprets this worsening situation as the "Lord's mystery"[17] and seeks to raise even more money to buy access to more internet sources. The father may be taken as a premillennialist, who wants to accelerate the path to the end in his pioneering of the world of simulations. The story shows the crisis of digitalization, in other words the "digital crisis," which is an apocalyptic anxiety dynamically presented in the play. Pete's idea that shopping through regular physical means is not necessary as there is "a [TV] channel for groceries, a channel for meals …" now available to shop through, confirms that digital means are replacing the regular ways of doing even daily activities.[18] More examples of this digital crisis can be found in the play, paving one of the

13 Ravenhill, *Plays 1*, 97.
14 Ibid., 97.
15 Ibid., 96.
16 Ibid., 121.
17 Ibid., 121.
18 Ibid., 122.

ways for the apocalyptic tone of the play. Pete's or Donny's means of communication through the internet,[19] and Pete's creating a homepage for himself on the internet[20] are among such illustrations. Forming a virtual life and filtering and avoiding real life experiences through screens, as in the case of Pete, is also a symptom of personal internal crisis, which contributes more to the play's critical atmosphere after the external crisis of the world has been presented. Pete and Donny's competition in scarring their bodies, which immediately turns out to be a death game, is an indicator of the internal crisis of the characters, too. A third indication of the same would be found in Pete's trying to rush Alain to leave the motel room and keep running throughout the country, to escape some sort of "they."[21] The instances that add up to the sense of crisis in the play are many. Even in the last seconds of the play, the crisis remains active: the "beeping" sound in the last scene,[22] referring to the heartbeats and signalling the last moments of Alain's life, radiates a no less critical tone than the highly crisis-laden opening speech of Chorus at the beginning of the play.

Apart from a severe sense of crisis, which prepares the background for the apocalyptic rhetoric, a perception of chaos, the cessation of established systems of reality, the end of emotional life, the representation of life lived through a left-over body, and a sense of imminent catastrophe are other apocalyptic representations generally found in In-Yer-Face theatre, and particularly present in *Faust Is Dead*. This second successful play of Ravenhill, like his *Shopping and F***ing*, is entirely filled with apocalyptic resonances. The major character of the play, Alain, is based on Michel Foucault and Jean Baudrillard, whose philosophies relating to the end of History, the death of Man, and the end of reality have been very influential. After the initial speech of Chorus, which may be seen as a prologue, the play opens with a TV show managed by a late-night talk-show figure, David Letterman, hosting both Madonna and Alain, the interest being on the former guest while the latter is treated ironically due to his book called *The Death of Man* …, throughout which Alain problematizes the death of Man "as an idea, as a construct."[23] Therefore, the apocalyptic vein, right after Chorus' speech of a world in crisis, is triggered at the very beginning of the play through Alain's thought-provoking book. What is more, it is also made clear that Alain is

19 Ibid., 122.
20 Ibid., 123.
21 Ibid., 136.
22 Ibid., 139.
23 Ibid., 98.

not exempt from what he preaches in his book since he himself appears suicidal, as he is thinking of his own death. After being warned by "Ms. Brannigan – the Director of Studies" of his department – for telling a story offensive to a possible sponsor from Japan, and hence causing the candidate's dislike, Alain cannot help responding to Ms. Brannigan in a very rude way, after which he "decided that maybe I should live a little."[24] Alain seems to be forlorn. His narration of the story which offends the Japanese candidate for sponsorship to some extent demonstrates why he writes a book of apocalyptic content and why he feels so suicidal: "In 1981 a Dutch woman was on business in Tokyo, when she met a Japanese businessman. He invited her to join him for a meal. She read him some of her poetry. While she was reading, he shot her. Several times. He then chopped her up, put her in his bowl and ate her."[25] This is Alain's first story (there will be several others) relating to the death of Man. Structurally speaking, the play starts immediately with Chorus' emphatic expression that "the world is such a bad place,"[26] and what follows in the rest, with Alain's story exemplifying why he may be thinking that mankind is dead, and his depressive attitude, promises a revelation and a clarification of Chorus' initial idea about the wickedness in the world.

The next point to shed light on the apocalyptic spirit of the play arises with Alain's comparison between America and Europe. His major point of contrast between the two lands is related to the quality of liveliness of these lands. Alain considers America as a land of dynamism, a last stand for vivacity in the twentieth century as he says (in French): "For me, and for so many children of this twentieth century, it is only in America that we really believe that we are alive, that we are living within in our own century."[27] On the other hand, he sees Europe as a dead, departed, and lifeless terrain when he says (in French): "In Europe, we are ghosts, trapped in a museum, with the lights out and the last visitor long gone."[28] Besides, Alain's uttering of all these words in French contributes more to the notion of the end of Europe and the notion of America as the land of life since French, according to Alain's observation, can be seen as an ancient language reminiscent of a time of civilization, which no longer has the vigor it used to have. That European civilization has come to its end, opening ways up to the new land

24 Ibid., 99.
25 Ibid., 99.
26 Ibid., 97.
27 Ibid., 101.
28 Ibid.

of life in America, and is obviously full of apocalyptic reverberations. Of course, the deceased Europe Alain mentions should not be understood as a total void and chaos with an entire barren land where nothing lives, grows, or regenerates. Life goes on in Europe, but the quality of life is the poorest ever, linking it to the idea that a post-apocalyptic phase of life has remained in Europe. What Chorus has stated in terms of crisis throughout the world at the beginning of the play, on the other hand, reveals that America should not be understood as a heavenly place but rather a location in crisis of the now and here before its ultimate end. This may explain why the play is deliberately set in "the west coast of America"[29] and why Alain came to live in America. In scene seven, Chorus' narration of the event of the "whole city's blowing right apart," or Pete's eye-witnessing "[guys] looting shops, guys burning cars, guys burning guys,"[30] referring to a civil crisis of riots and vandalism due to the absence of food as one of the causes in one of the American cities, proves the feeling of the nearing end for America. More, the personification of America with Pete and of Europe with Alain is also notable. The pairs are perfect matches as the lively character of Pete with his singing, though in grunge style with words full of hatred, suits Alain's description of America as the land of life, while Alain fits into his depiction of Europe as a ghostly and forsaken land, in his drunkenness and with his constant studies and stories about the end of life. Jean Baudrillard in "The Anorexic Ruins" says:

> Something escapes us; we escape ourselves in a process of no return, we have missed a certain point for turning back, a certain point of the contradiction in things, and have entered a universe of noncontradiction alive, of blind rapture, of ecstasy, of amazement about the irreversible processes that nevertheless have no direction at all.[31]

What Baudrillard is defining above can be called the state of chaos. The perception of chaos as the oncoming state of life is, thus, another point to be mentioned. *Faust Is Dead* is loaded with a sense of emerging chaos. Pete's father Bill (referring to Bill Gates), leading a big company in the production and marketing of software, created a new computer programme – "chaos" in Pete's words[32] – with which he is planning to take control of each household. Showing Alain the only copy of this programme, which he stole from his father, Pete explains everything

29 Ibid., 96.

30 Ibid., 107.

31 Jean Baudrillard, "The Anorexic Ruins," trans. David Antal, in Looking Back on the End of the World, edited by Dietmar Kamper, Christoph Wulf (New York: Semiotext(e), 1989), 32.

32 Ravenhill, *Plays 1*, 110.

about it to him: “This is chaos. Only copy in the world. See, my dad’s seen the future and he knows how to give his product the lead for like centuries into the new millennium. Chaos is the answer.”[33] Chaos here implies the post-apocalyptic phase of life which will replace the present critical phase of life once an apocalyptic breakthrough occurs.

Faust Is Dead premiered just four years before the end of the twentieth century and the advent of the next millennium which was historically been considered an apocalyptic overturning. Reflecting this historical mood in the real world, Pete’s chaos software and its activation in “the new millennium” has entirely millennialist and apocalyptic overtones. Furthermore, Alain’s lecture about the end of History and the new phase of life is also remarkable in terms of the perception of chaos in the play. Alain, as a university professor, starts:

> ALAIN: I call this moment the End of History because what we understood as history, this movement forward, has ended. And the words which have for so been our guides … Progress, for example. This now means nothing. We know this in our hearts. Every man, every woman, they know it, they feel, but they don’t say it. So we have to ask ourselves this question: When will we embrace … (this is a word for you also, embrace?) … chaos … When will we live the End of History? When will we live in our time? And how will we live in this new age of chaos? Not as we lived in the old age. Not with the old language. Not by being more kind, more … enlightened.[34]

The speech mirrors Lee Quinby’s “ironic apocalypse,” which sees apocalypse as a phenomenon that will come after the history will have used up time, and not bring rebirth or refreshment.[35] Alain proclaims the end of History, the end of the course of regular and linear times, which have moved ever forward alongside human-made progress. More, he claims that people are aware of this fact but prefer to keep it unpublicized. In this speech his questions about when to actualize the end of History point directly to the expected apocalyptic break, which will steer mankind into a phase of life ruled, or rather unruled, by chaos. Chaos is going to replace the present conditions of life and, hence, what follows will be a post-apocalyptic period of survival and existence. Chaos here may be perceived as a stage of life in a disorderly mess while it may also be understood as an abyss pregnant with everything from the beginning. The first reading would be a modern-day interpretation of chaos while the latter could be rooted in classical

33 Ibid., 110.

34 Ibid., 120–121.

35 Lee Quinby, Anti-apocalypse: Exercises in Genealogical Criticism (Minneapolis: University of Minnesota Press, 1994), xvi.

mythology, whose myths of creation, whether Homeric, Pelasgian, or Olympian preach that in the beginning there was chaos.[36] All in all, the use of chaos as the next phase of life, whether as in the contemporary use of "disorderliness" or as in the mythological "beginning," entirely matches the apocalyptic spirit of *Faust Is Dead.*

The appearance of Donny in scene fourteen strengthens Alain's apocalyptic chaos theory. Alain completes his lecture to Pete about the end of History and the forthcoming period of chaos with the following words: "We must be cruel, we must follow our desires and be cruel to others, yes, but also we must be cruel to ourselves. We must embrace suffering, we must embrace cruelty."[37] According to Alain, embracing cruelty and suffering is the way to open the gates of chaos. "Not with the old language" of the traditional regular times, which consisted of the religious teachings, human-made laws, value and belief systems, pursuit after rights, waging wars and looking for peace, and so on, but with the new awareness that an internalization of cruelty and suffering is key to the new life of chaos. In this sense, Donny is the perfect anti-hero, who embraces suffering. In his embracing suffering through his cutting his body, he even compares himself to Jesus Christ, taking the apocalyptic tone one step further: "Jesus had quite a few cuts too by the end and I reckon he understands why I do this to myself. I like Jesus, although I never met him. But I believe it's possible."[38] Donny is a character who leads his life on webpages and tries to concretize his abstracted life through physical violence to himself. Donny's masochism (without sexual motives), thus, is violently apocalyptic. Immediately after Alain sees Donny on the internet, he is spellbound by this live demonstration of his theories of the end of History, the death of Man and the inauguration of chaos, and he calls what he sees in Donny as "beautiful."[39] Further mesmerized, Alain sees what Donny has achieved by willfully cutting his body as "a testament of suffering upon the body" and announces the act as "an initiation rite for the end of the twentieth century."[40] Donny is Alain's theories incarnate, in his attempt to bring the end of the linear and traditional time by embracing suffering.

Another apocalyptic motif can be found in the use of the desert as a setting, where some parts of the play (starting with scene ten) take place. A desert, as a

36 Robert Graves, Greek Myths (London: Penguin Books, 1992), 27–33.
37 Ravenhill, *Plays 1*, 121.
38 Ibid., 130.
39 Ibid., 123.
40 Ibid., 124.

location, immediately recalls the notions of barrenness, drought, unproductiveness, sterility, isolation, inaccessibility and, in general, nothingness. It is easily associable with a place where decay is the natural law of order, turning even the objects of nature into minute particles. Therefore, the desert, where "[nothing] beside remains" as Shelley writes in his "Ozymandias," is, by its nature, an apocalyptic place.[41] Alain and Pete set off on a trip, escaping from the city, and they end up near "Death Valley"[42] in the desert, where Alain wants to engage in homosexual relations with Pete. The name of the valley, too, contributes to the already apocalyptic atmosphere of the desert. Alain, despite all its nihility, finds the desert pleasant and says, "[this] is a very beautiful place,"[43] an indication which strengthens the idea of Alain's fascination with the end of things. Pete, on the other hand, is numbed to experiences of any kind, even of the sexual kind as he does not "feel a thing,"[44] and is even unaware of his own orgasm at the end of Alain's homophile activity. The desert, hence, with all its nihility provides these two characters of uneasy psychology with a new opportunity "to have an experience" of reality, for which they try to "shape the experience" by using drugs.[45] Theirs is an attempt to vitalize and regain their ability to feel real experiences. Ravenhill's use of the desert is not casual. Jean Baudrillard at the beginning of his *Simulacra and Simulation* uses a metaphor of the desert to explain the relation between the loss of the real and its replacement with hyperreality:

> Abstraction today is no longer that of the map, the double, the mirror, or the concept. Simulation is no longer that of a territory, a referential being, or a substance. It is the generation by models of a real without origin or reality: a hyperreal. The territory no longer precedes the map, nor does it survive it … It is the real, and not the map, whose vestiges subsist here and there, in the deserts which are no longer those of the Empire, but our own. The desert of the real itself.[46]

The captivation of Alain's mind with the idea of the end of everything, combined with their search for real experiences in the middle of the desert, together with Pete's aloofness from sex prepares the mood in the play for one of the most apocalyptic speeches, which comes from Alain: "Man is dead, you know. And Progress. Progress also. Progress is dead. And Humanity. Yes. Humanity

41 Percy Bysshe Shelley, Shelley: Poems (London: Penguin Books, 1956), 107.
42 Ravenhill, *Plays 1*, 114.
43 Ibid., 113.
44 Ibid., 115.
45 Ibid., 116.
46 Jean Baudrillard, Simulacra and Simulation (Ann Arbor: University of Michigan Press, 1994), 1.

is dead."[47] With the repetition of the words, terseness of expression and the abrupt pauses that disperse meaning, the speech is as apocalyptic as it can be since it announces the end of the image of humankind as well as its civilization. By "Man" Alain signifies man "as an idea"[48] and by "Humanity" he means the gist of the idea, which have both met their demise. This also accords with Nietzschean prophecy in his *Thus Spoke Zarathustra*, where it is claimed that "[the] human is something that shall be overcome."[49] The end of Man has killed the senses, and that of humanity has terminated feelings, thereby making it almost impossible for the left-over man of the end of the twentieth century to have either sensual or emotional experiences. Aware of this fact, Pete and Alain respond to Alain's apocalyptic manifesto by continuing their search for experience of reality through homosexual stimulation under the effect of narcotic drugs in the middle of a desert.

The Baudrillardian end of reality is no less problematized throughout *Faust Is Dead* than the Foucauldian death of Man or the end of History. It is shown in two complementary veins: the end of real experiences and the beginning of a virtual world. Already Pete and Alain have been suffering from inability to attain real experiences, as we have seen. Again, already Pete's recording everything he sees or experiences on a camcorder, and the chaos software he held as the key power source for the next phase of life, implied the turn of the times into more digital spheres. Donny's appearance in scene fourteen, however, intensifies both issues. Communication between Donny and Pete as well as among many other users is made possible through digital means on the internet. Donny is an internet personage and expresses himself through it. Donny's way of digital expression, harbouring the idea of the beginning of a digitalized world, is combined with the end of real experiences, as the way Donny expresses himself through the internet is by opening cuts and scars on his own body; it is a search, like Alain's and Pete's (and even Gary's in *Shopping and F***ing*), to find the taste of real experiences, or "a desperate way of making contact with reality."[50] At some point Alain and Pete discuss and question even the reality of Donny as he appears on the screen:

---

47 Ravenhill, *Plays 1*, 117.

48 Ibid., 98.

49 Friedrich Nietzsche, Thus Spoke Zarathustra (New York: Oxford University Press, 2005), 11.

50 Dan Reballato, "Introduction," in *Plays 1: Shopping and F***ing, Faust Is Dead, Handbag, Some Explicit Polaroids*, edited by Mark Ravenhill (London: Methuen Drama, 2001), xvi.

ALAIN: Hello, Donny. Donny – you there?
PETE: Hey, listen. Listen, Donny is a fake.
ALAIN: I don't think so.
PETE: No. I don't … I don't believe this.
Look at this guy. It's not for real.
ALAIN: He seems real.[51]

Donny, on the other hand, tries to express his reality when he says: "<I'M NO FAKE. I'M FOR REAL.>."[52] To prove that he exists and is real, he even proposes that Alain and Pete meet him personally, which they accept. In the meantime, seeing Alain's infatuation with Donny, Pete grows jealous of Donny. That is why when Donny arrives, Pete offers him to have a "who's got the best"[53] cut competition for which Alain, who has been recording since Donny came in, to be judge. First Pete "cuts across his chest" and he feels "Pure. Clear. True"[54] as a result. When it is Donny's turn, he suddenly "cuts his jugular,"[55] and dies on the spot. Donny ends his life because he "had enough of just communicating … in a virtual kind of way,"[56] as Chorus reports from Donny's earlier words. Donny's unexpected suicide leads Alain to a mental transcendence, and he philosophizes on the end of reality with the following words: "At some point, at a moment at the end of the twentieth century, reality ended. Reality finished and simulation began."[57] Therefore, what Alain openly declares points out that all examples in the play relating to the virtual quality of life suggest the fact that the traditional sense of reality has come to an end and is superseded by virtual reality. After the end of the traditional reality, it is now a post-mortem state of life in which sensual as well as emotional experiences are denied to people. It is a post-mortem state of reality since "Reality died. It ended" and the present virtual state of life is a "dream" or a "lie" or a "simulated existence,"[58] as Alain claims. All these claims relating to the end of reality match Jean Baudrillard's philosophies in his book *Simulacra and Simulation*, where he maintains that the traditional sense of reality, in other words, the reality whose objects would match their signs and

51 Ravenhill, *Plays 1*, 125.
52 Ibid.
53 Ibid., 130.
54 Ibid., 131.
55 Ibid.
56 Ibid., 134.
57 Ibid., 132.
58 Ibid., 132.

appeal to senses has been replaced by a sense of hyperreality,[59] "because there is no longer anything real to reflect."[60]

More darkly apocalyptic compared to Foucault's ideas of the end, Baudrillard asserts that the phenomenon of reality has passed through a transition and died, leaving its place to hyperreal; and its dissolution occurred in four steps: in the first of these the image of reality reflects the basic reality. This is followed by a phase of the image of reality when it covers and shadows the basic reality. The third step occurred when the image masked the absence of basic reality, giving way to the last step and the inauguration of hyperreal when it has lost all contact with reality.[61] Baudrillard comments on these four steps with the following words:

> In the first case, the image is a *good* appearance – representation is of the sacramental order. In the second, it is an evil appearance – it is of the order of maleficence. In the third, it plays at being an appearance – it is of the order of sorcery. In the fourth, it is no longer of the order of appearances, but of simulation.[62]

Alain understands all these since he is a philosopher. Pete is a learner and Alain's student, who realizes the transition only to escape to the safer side, to his father's hyperreal kingdom, instead of trying to challenge it. Donny is helplessly living in the fourth phase in a hyperreal world, where the referents of life are only virtual, and it is surrounded by a cyber-atmosphere. It is impossible for him to free himself from the net of hyperreality that tightens itself more and more and turn back to the earlier phases of reality.

Chorus has grown weary of the happenings of the present life and comes up with the most explicitly apocalyptic excerpt of the play, in scene eighteen:

> CHORUS: Looking back, now I'm an adult, I think I used to cry at night not because the world was such a bad place. Well, okay, not just because the world is such a bad place. But also because I wanted the world to come to an end. Like Armageddon or Hellfire or Total Meltdown or some such catastrophe. And I cried because I felt so guilty because it was gonna happen any day and it would be all my fault for wanting it so much. But the world hasn't ended. It's going on and on. And I keep on looking for signs that it's getting better like Momma told me. But I can't see them. So, it hasn't ended and it's not getting better. It's just going on, on and on and on. And I wonder if I should feel something about that. But – you want the truth? – I don't feel a thing. See, I'm the kind of person

---

59 Baudrillard, Simulacra and Simulation, 1–2.

60 Chris Snipp-Walmsley, "Postmodernism," in Literary Theory and Criticism, ed*ited by Patricia Waugh* (Oxford: Oxford University Press, 2006), 413.

61 Baudrillard, Simulacra and Simulation, 6.

62 Ibid., 6.

> who can stand in the middle of an earthquake and I'm just like "whoa, neat earthquake." And I wonder what made me that way.[63]

This speech, which is uttered almost at the end of the play, finalizes all the apocalyptic echoes that the play has been reflecting since its beginning. It displays the gist of all the ideas issued in the play, like the death of Man, the end of History, the end of reality, the age of chaos, and the age of virtual reality. Chorus here unequivocally claims that the main reason why he would cry when he was a child was that he wished that the world would come to an end through some sort of catastrophic occurrences. Chorus's visions as a child render the apocalypticism of his idea doubly apocalyptic as it is a child's imagining of the end of the world with a catastrophe, a child being presumably, or at least conventionally, the most innocent of human beings. Chorus' wish has not been actualized as he imagined, but it is possible that he has been experiencing the end of Man, of History, and of reality for the most part of the twentieth century. Therefore, it is possible to claim also for Chorus' speech that the present world depicted in *Faust Is Dead* is a post-apocalyptic world. The expectation of an apocalypse as prophesied by the religious books has proved a loss of time since the end has already come during the twentieth century, and what has been lived since then is a post-apocalyptic world of ends. Therefore, Chorus could not see his wish of a huge catastrophe smashing the world come true but, on the contrary, the world continued to deteriorate giving birth to people who cannot feel or are deprived of real-life experiences. This is why the Chorus has turned numb and cannot "feel a thing"[64] or care if there has been an earthquake. It is also possible to detect one part of Derridean apocalypticism hidden in this speech: "the end of the ends" or "la fin de la fin"[65] is observable in Chorus' assertion that the world is "just going on and on and on and on."[66]

"Because man is dead. For so many centuries, we have believed in his existence. This thing, this construct, this thing we called man. But one day, some day in the twentieth century, he went and died … God died and we trembled to live in a universe without him."[67] These words uttered by Pete are the opening expressions of the last scene of *Faust Is Dead*. As well as confirming what the

63 Ravenhill, *Plays 1*, 137.

64 Ibid.

65 Jacques Derrida, "Of an Apocalyptic Tone Recently Adopted in Philosophy, trans. J.P. Leavey, Oxford Literary Review 6, no:2 (1984): 21.

66 Ravenhill, *Plays 1*, 137.

67 Ibid., 138.

previous parts of the play thematized in relation to the end, this final section brings up an extra issue of the death of Man in the twentieth century: the transformation of Man from subject to object. The theory again belongs to Michel Foucault, who philosophized on such a transformation in his book *The Order of Things*. He claimed that Man, throughout the twentieth century, due to technological progress and high levels of production came to be defined by the objects he himself produced, turning into "an instrument of production."[68] Frederic Jameson, too, observes the dissolution of the subject when he writes:

> ... Today, from any number of distinct perspectives, the social theorists, the psychoanalysts, even the linguists, not to speak of those of us who work in the area of culture and cultural and formal change, are all exploring the notion that that kind of individualism and personal identity is a thing of the past; that the old individual or individualist subject is "dead" ...[69]

These theories find their echo in Pete's words: "But now we see, we feel that we are no longer the subject but the object of forces, we are a confusion, a collision ..."[70] Therefore, it is the time of the *postman*, a term which should be understood to signify the new form of Man as a confusion, or rather a fusion, and a collision of its self and its productions. In fact, what Pete has been practicing as behaviors are all excerpts from Alain's book. This recalls a master-pupil relation like the one between Socrates and Plato. Pete the Plato prophecies that "the next millennium will see the fight between those who embrace and those who deny the death of man,"[71] for which Pete and his father would fall into the clique of the deniers whereas Alain, Chorus and Donny would be listed in the embracing group. Although the majority of the people represented by Chorus seem to be on the side that confirms the death of Man, the fight will still be harsh since Bill and Pete will be the power holders of society – as Donny predicts, speaking of Pete and his father: "Gone to his daddy and they're gonna take over the world."[72] Pete has decided to join his father and help him in his business, failing in his search for real life experiences, and choosing to go on living in the virtual world. He prefers living Baudrillard's depiction of simulated experiences of the digital

68 Michel Foucault, *The Order of Things: An Archeology of Human Sciences* (New York: Vintage Books, 1994), 313.

69 Frederic Jameson, "Postmodernism and Consumer Society: The Death of the Subject," in *The Norton Anthology of Theory and Criticism*, edited by Vincent B. Leitch (New York: W.W. Norton & Company, 2001), 1960..

70 Ravenhill, *Plays 1*, 138.

71 Ibid.

72 Ibid., 140.

world, as he heartily advertises his father's virtual solutions on the programmable modifications of moods that paintings can give the viewers according to their moods.[73] As such, Pete proves one of the most apocalyptic philosophies found in the play.

Alain's last words are "I don't want to get better,"[74] meaning that he would rather die than live in the none-get-better world. The play comes to close with the appearance of Donny without eyes, hence making up a shocking ending that blends the verisimilitude of the play with the fantastic thriller mode. *Faust Is Dead* is a play written as an imitation of classical plays and the very ending of it, as well as the presence of Chorus all throughout, is reminiscent of the tradition; Donny here, and his reference to "the boat to heaven,"[75] are derived from the classical myth of the Boatman Charon who, on his boat and in return for coins placed on each eye of the deceased, carries the dead to the other side of the underworld. The mythological underworld, still, suggests a new beginning for the deceased souls. However, *Faust Is Dead* ends apocalyptically so darkly that Donny cannot find an end even after he is dead. Although, he commits suicide to bring the end of himself, and therefore find an existence in death, he is denied a new beginning in the other life. Chorus's words "it hasn't ended and it's not getting better. It's just going on, on and on and on"[76] now resonate more emphatically at the end of the play. These words also signify that the end is not attainable, reminding one of and matching Baudrillard's following words in his *The Illusion of the End*: "Things are in a state which is literally definitive – neither finished, nor infinite, nor definite, but de-finitive that is, deprived of its end."[77] At the end of the play all characters are deprived of the real experience of the end.

Conclusion

Considering all the above-mentioned arguments, we can reach the conclusion that *Faust Is Dead* is a play which makes a powerful contribution to the apocalypticism found in In-Yer-Face plays of the 1990s. Endowed with a title that announces the end of one of the most significant and archetypal characters of the European culture – Faust – with an atmosphere of crisis that stretches from

73 Ibid., 139–140.

74 Ibid., 140.

75 Ibid., 140.

76 Ibid., 137.

77 Jean Baudrillard, *The Illusion of the End*, trans. Chris Turner (Stanford: Stanford University Press, 1994), 120.

global to individual levels and that paves the way for the apocalyptic rhetoric, with the ideas problematized around the issues like an emerging chaos, the cessation of established systems of reality, the emotional apathy, the digitalization of life, the death of Europe and a sense of imminent catastrophe for America, the play is a dramaturgical rewriting of some of the most influential apocalyptic theories of the twentieth century like Foucauldian end of History, the death of Man, and the change of the order of subject and object in the century due to the advances in technological world and progress in production, and Baudrillardian end of reality and the commencement of the virtual world of hyperreality. All in all, with all its direct references and allusions to all these ideas, the apocalypticism of *Faust Is Dead* by Mark Ravenhill is a philosophical apocalypse.

Bibliography

Baudrillard, Jean. "The Anorexic Ruins." Translated by David Antal. In *Looking Back on the End of the World*, edited by Dietmar Kamper and Christoph Wulf. New York: Semiotext(e), 1989: 29–45

Baudrillard, Jean. *Simulacra and Simulation*. Ann Arbor: University of Michigan Press, 1994a.

Baudrillard, Jean. *The Illusion of the End*. Translated by Chris Turner. Stanford: Stanford University Press, 1994b.

Derrida, Jacques. "Of an Apocalyptic Tone Recently Adopted in Philosophy." Translated by J.P. Leavey. *Oxford Literary Review* 6, no. 2 (1984): 3–37.

Foucault, Michel. *The Order of Things: An Archeology of Human Sciences*. New York: VintageBooks, 1994.

Graves, Robert. *Greek Myths*. London: Penguin Books, 1992.

Jameson, Frederic. "Postmodernism and Consumer Society: The Death of the Subject." In *The Norton Anthology of Theory and Criticism*, edited by Vincent B. Leitch. New York: W.W. Norton & Company, 2001: 1960–1974.

Nietzsche, Friedrich. *Thus Spoke Zarathustra*. New York: Oxford University Press, 2005.

Quinby, Lee. *Anti-apocalypse: Exercises in Genealogical Criticism*. Minneapolis: University of Minnesota Press, 1994.

Ravenhill, Mark. *Plays 1: Shopping and F***ing, Faust Is Dead, Handbag, Some Explicit Polaroids*. London: Methuen Drama, 2001.

Ravenhill, Mark. "Mark Ravenhill." Interview by Enric Monforte. *British Theatre of the 1990s: Interviews with Directors, Playwrights, Critics and Academics*, edited by Mireia Aragay, Hildegard Klein, Enric Monforte, and Pilar Zozoya. New York: Palgrave Macmillan, 2007: 91–104.

Rebellato, Dan. “Introduction.” In *Plays 1: Shopping and F***ing, Faust Is Dead, Handbag, Some Explicit Polaroids*, edited by Mark Ravenhill. London: Methuen Drama, 2001: ix–xx.

Shelley, Percy Bysshe. *Shelley: Poems*. London: Penguin Books, 1956.

Sierz, Aleks. *In-Yer-Face Theatre: British Drama Today*. London: Faber and Faber, 2000.

Snipp-Walmsley, Chris. “Postmodernism.” In *Literary Theory and Criticism*, edited by PatriciaWaugh. Oxford: Oxford University Press, 2006: 405–426.

Özlem Karadağ

Becoming Human/oid: A Posthumanist Critique of Thomas Eccleshare's *Instructions for Correct Assembly*

Thomas Eccleshare's *Instructions for Correct Assembly* is directed by Hamish Pirie and first performed in 2018 at Royal Court Theatre. Although at its core the play is about the trauma of losing a son, the specific choice of competing with loss by purchasing a flatpack humanoid and the addiction to anthropocentric progress and perfection provide fertile ground for a posthumanist critique of the play. While the play shows that the humanoid, Jån, is transformed into a marginalized and colonized other, it also unfolds a desire of becoming human on Jån's side, and becoming machine on Max and Hari's side, however, not in a Braidottian way. Thus, in the light of Rosi Braidotti's philosophy of the Posthuman, becoming and hybridity in Eccleshare's play become central to a critical posthumanist reading.

"What Is Posthumanism?"[1]

Posthumanism, similar to humanism, is a complex term and interpreted in different ways by oppositional posthumanist thinkers/scientists. Tamar Sharon suggests that there are "four different types of posthumanist discourse […] a 'dystopic', a 'liberal', a 'radical' and a 'methodological' posthumanism."[2] Joel Garreau indicates that for liberal posthumanists or transhumanists, "posthuman" is the point humanity will eventually reach, transhumanism is a transitional stage before becoming a posthuman, and transhumanists are "keen on the enhancement of human intellectual, physical and emotional capabilities, the elimination of disease and unnecessary suffering[…]."[3] The limitless*ness* of bio/technology

1 "What is posthumanism?" is not only the name of Cary Wolfe's seminal work, but it is also a question posed many times by authors such as Braidotti, Bostrom.

2 Tamar Sharon, *Human Nature in an Age of Biotechnology: The Case for Mediated Posthumanism* (Dordrecht: Springer, 2014), 5.

3 Joel Garreau. *Radical Evolution: The Promise and Peril of Enhancing Our Minds, Our Bodies and What It Means to Be Human* (New York: Broadway Books, 2005), chap. 7, Kindle.

is the source of dystopic visions for thinkers such as Fukuyama and of transhumanist/liberal visions for thinkers such as Nick Bostrom whose definition of the posthuman is broadly "possible future beings whose basic capacities so radically exceed those of present humans as to be no longer unambiguously human by our current standards" as they may have many different mental capabilities.[4] Thus, it can be understood that transhumanism, which aims at becoming posthuman through the enhancement of the human mind, leaves the body behind and disregards other species.

However, radical posthumanism, a discourse created and followed by philosophers such as Braidotti and Haraway, criticizes this disembodied and anthropocentric attitude of transhumanism. They argue that a disembodied future aims the enhancement of the human mind and its impact on our environment. Thus, it moves Renaissance humanism, Enlightenment ideology, and Cartesian duality dramatically forward. Tony Davies suggests that Renaissance humanism, "expressive of an essential humanity unconditioned by time, place or circumstance, is a nineteenth-century anachronism"[5] and "separate*s* out and privilege*s* 'Man' [...]."[6] Rosi Braidotti is "not fond of" this exclusionary Humanism, and the transhumanist Posthuman that derives from it. Although "[t]he potential medical benefits are too many to list,"[7] it pushes us towards a disembodied, technologically advanced and hybridized future that still reinforces human superiority over the others. Therefore, she offers an anti-humanist, critical posthumanism "from *her* own tradition of anti-humanist philosophies of subjectivity."[8]

Braidotti, cultivating postcolonial, post-feminist, and post-structuralist philosophy and molding them into her philosophy of the posthuman, offers, as a solution, the Posthuman as Becoming Other.[9] The idea of becoming, tackled in her *Metamorphoses* and *the Posthuman*, is rooted in "Deleuze's multiple subjects

4 Nick Bostrom, *The Transhumanist FAQ* (World Transhumanist Association, 2003): 5–6, "https://www.nickbostrom.com/views/transhumanist.pdf.

5 Tony Davies, *Humanism* (London: Routledge, 1997), 25.

6 Ibid., 25. My italics.

7 Bostrom, *Transhumanist FAQ*, 7.

8 Rosi Braidotti, *The Posthuman* (Cambridge: Polity Press, 2013), 38.

9 Ibid., 55–104. (She talks about becoming woman/animal/insect/Earth/machine in *Metamorphoses* and *the Posthuman*, I wanted to refer to all of them as the other moving from her aim to deconstruct the centrality of the humanist idea of man as the measure of everything which has lead to the marginalization of women, indigenous people, nonhuman animals and other than human beings.)

of becoming"[10] and with a materialist approach, she contemplates upon subjectivity and investigates becoming woman, animal, insect, machine, animal, and Earth. All of which is the required natural responses to a future of peaceful, post-anthropocentric co-existence.

Deleuzian and Guattarian becoming, imitation, and rhizome theory are all important in understanding the nature of theatre as well as Braidotti's use of them. Becoming, as explained in Deleuze's and Guattari, is "an emphasis on becoming rather than being."[11] It is also about deterritorialization and multiplicity: "Each of these becomings brings about the deterritorialization of one term and the reterritorialization of the other."[12] Deterritorialization and reterritorialization is not about changing or replacing the other, but it is an attempt at multiplicity. Their rhizome theory is also important to Braidottian becoming and multiplicity because although Deleuze and Guattari acknowledge the importance of imitation, they also clearly indicate that "[b]ecoming is never imitating."[13] The rhizome offers a theory of existence that works upon the principle of heterogeneity, connection as parallel co-existence, multiplicity, and "asignifying rupture."[14] Deleuze and Guattari see all organic and inorganic entities as bodies that comprise different materials or organisms thus existing according to the rhizome theory.

Therefore, the deterritorialization of human is not for the sake of replacing it with something other than human, but as Braidotti also embraces, the aim is the realization of the rhizomatic theory of life that shows us the principle of multiplicity and co-existence, and not only for the organic beings: "not all Life is confined to the organic strata: [...] there is a life all the more intense, all the more powerful for being anorganic. There are also nonhuman Becomings of human beings that overspill the anthropomorphic strata in all directions."[15] In the same vein, the pieces that bring them together make machines images of multiplicity, and for Deleuze and Guattari "[e]verything is a

---

10 Rosi Braidotti, *Metamorphoses: Towards a Material Theory of Becoming* (Cambridge: Polity, 2002), 7.

11 Claire Colebrook, *Gilles Deleuze* (London: Routledge, 2002), 8.

12 Gilles Deleuze and Felix Guattari, *A Thousand Plateaus: Capitalism and Schizophrenia* (Minneapolis: Minneapolis University Press, 2005), 10.

13 Ibid., 305.

14 Ibid., 7–9.

15 Ibid., 503.

machine."[1617] In any case, machines – desiring machines, bodies without organs – have more than inorganic ties with nature and organic beings because as Braidotti suggests "[t]he human organism is neither wholly human, nor just an organism. It is an abstract machine, which captures, transforms and produces interconnections."[18]

The rhizome and producing interconnections are also foundational in Braidotti's concept of Art. Talking about Art, she suggests that "Art does not imitate: […] This is a process of becoming that deterritorializes both the artist and his or her object. Against imitation, rhizomatic music aims at deterritorializing our acoustic habits, making us aware that the human is not the ruling principle in the harmony of the spheres."[19] Moving from her idea of Art as a process of becoming, it can be suggested that theatre is rhizomatic as it is an Art form based upon the co-existence of various forms and agencies (bringing together mimesis, language, other semiotic and symbolic referents, gestures, mimics) and producing interconnections.

Braidotti argues that Art is "an intensive practice that aims at creating new ways of thinking, perceiving and sensing Life's infinite possibilities" and by "transposing us beyond the confines of bound identities, art becomes necessarily inhuman […] it connects to the animal, the vegetable, earthy and planetary forces that surround us. Art is also […] posthuman by structure, as it carries us to the limits of what our embodied selves can do or endure."[20] In the same vein,

---

16 Gilles Deleuze and Felix Guattari, *Anti-Oedipus: Capitalism and Schizophrenia* (Minneapolis: Minneapolis University Press, 2000), 2.

17 This can either be seen as a parallelism to Lyotard's idea of humans as creations of technology or can be a way of reading organic bodies' movements and functions as mechanical. Lyotard's suggests that "[t]echnology wasn't invented by us humans. Rather the other way around. […] even the simplest life forms, […] are already technical devices." Furthermore, although I do not embrace Descartes' idea of animals as machines, when it is used to refer to human-animals as machines and when united with Lyotard's idea of humans as devices created by technology, it becomes easier to suggest that any in/organic system with the ability to use information can be seen as a machine.

Jean-François Lyotard, *The Inhuman*, Translated by Geoffrey Bennington and Rachel Bowlby (Stanford: Stanford University Press, 1991), 12.

René Descartes, "Discourse on Method," in *Discourse on Method and Meditations on First Philosophy*, Translated by Donald A. Cress (Indianapolis: Hackett Publishing Company, 1998), 31.

18 Braidotti, *Metamorphoses*, 226.

19 Ibid., 157.

20 Braidotti, *The Posthuman*, 107.

theatre is also a posthuman Art form, it both enables us to question our relationship with other beings and connects us with them. Thus, it has the potential to help us understand our environment and our companion species.

What Is Human/oid?[21]: *Instructions for Correct Assembly*

In *Social Robots from a Human Perspective*, Taipale suggests that Robots are looking more like human beings and not only in a physical sense of the word: "Since recent technical developments have made possible rather detailed technical mimicking of human beings and their social features, and incorporating them in silicon chips, there is a pronounced need to understand to what extent the humanness can be implanted in social robots. This is also an occasion to think over and discuss what the human is when considered in this context of social robots."[22] Robots, their capabilities, and our possible future are being reflected in the works of playwrights who aim to carry these questions onto the stage. Eccleshare's *Instructions for Correct Assembly* contemplates our posthuman future where humanoids turn into consumer objects serving anthropocentric purposes.

In the context of Eccleshare's play, Max and Hari, who buy a flatpack humanoid and end up placing chips on their heads, lay the foundation of humanity's transhumanist dreams. Jån, who reminds the audience of IKEA flatpack furniture, emerges as a criticism of our consumer society, because, for the market economy, technology is the recent hype.[23] As Braidotti suggests "[I]n the case of techno-bodies, the 'hype' is truly astonishing, considering that machines and humans have been interacting at all levels since the first industrial revolution."[24][25] In the

21 As a question posed by Braidotti "what is human" is a very important question that arises from a critical approach to the definition of human in our age, in the context of the play I chose to look at both ways.

22 Sakari Taipale et al., "Introduction: Situating the Human in Social Robots," in *Social Robots from a Human Perspective*, edited by Jane Vincent et al. (Heidelberg: Springer, 2015), 1.

23 The 2018 production of the play used Cal Dyfan's stage design, which placed a moving production line on the stage. The scenes such as Jån's assembly took place as scenes happening on this moving line. As mentioned before, the idea of a flatpack humanoid for domestic purposes is already a sign of consumerism and the stage design cleverly underlines this very idea, as well as being a reference to mechanization in an age of mass production.

24 Braidotti, *Metamorphoses*, 235–236.

25 It is influential here to remember Lyotard's idea of technology and Descartes' idea of animals as machines which I also interpret as humans as machines as mentioned above. Moving from these ideas, Braidotti's "techno-bodies" can be dated back to the

last decades, in their simplest forms, technological devices are more and more indispensable to our everyday lives as they are also becoming a part of, an extension of our bodies pointing out the formation of another kind of human machine. Moving from Braidotti's idea of Becoming Machine, it is possible to read Max and Hari's transformation as a failed attempt at becoming machine, and Jån the humanoid as a desiring machine that experiences becoming human.

Max and Hari buy the humanoid to be able to cope with the death of their son Nick, yet also, to try their luck at being perfect parents or having the perfect son, as Eccleshare suggests in a Royal Court interview.[26] Similar to the cross-dressings in Shakespeare's plays, the same actor plays Nick and Jån without clear demarcations between the two characters. LePage suggests that "[m]achines, today, increasingly have the appearance, and possibly the reality, of life as well as coming to resemble the human being in terms of her physical looks, gestures, and general intelligence, such that the boundary between the human and the machine seems 'thoroughly ambiguous' and 'leaky', as Haraway attests."[27] As if to play with this idea, Eccleshare states that "Nick and Jån are played by the same actor, so to all intents and purposes are identical. As a result, at times there may be a tension, even confusion, about who we are watching."[28] Thus, this choice intends to blur the boundaries between the human and the humanoid as well as time and action. This uncanny resemblance challenges the audience's anthropocentric view of the stage along with their perception of the boundaries between humans and machines and underlines our transhumanist and consumerist technology that turns all beings into machines.

The play starts with Hari talking about the special offer for a "do it yourself type thing" which is cheap and would be fun to do together as they "did with the

---

beginnings of life on Earth. In *Metamorphoses*, similar to Lyotard, she also draws attention to the human capacity of processing information but underlines what distinguishes posthuman bodies, they "relentlessly reproduce themselves." Rosi Braidotti, *Metamorphoses*, 228.

26 Hamish Pirie and Thomas Eccleshare, "*Instructions for Correct Assembly* Flatpack Interview," by Royal Court Theatre, 2018, video, https://royalcourttheatre.com/whats-on/instructions/.

27 Louise Emma LePage, "Beyond Character: A Post/Humanist Approach to Modern Theatre" (PhD diss., Royal Holloway College, University of London, 2012), 64. https://pure.royalholloway.ac.uk/portal/files/6385784/phd_thesis_louise_lepage.pdf.

28 Thomas Eccleshare, *Instructions for Correct Assembly* (London: Oberon Books Ltd., 2018), 5.

upstairs bed."[29] A few moments later, the audience realizes that rather than a piece of furniture, Hari was talking about a do-it-yourself humanoid. Reading from an "inch-thick book of instructions"[30] they try to assemble the pieces. This scene is important on two levels, first, with references to the bed and working together to assemble the humanoid, it replicates the process of making a baby, thus, beclouds, once again, the difference between humans and machines. Secondly, as the male character, Hari, is the one who imposes this project, it is an important reference to male procreation, which does not necessitate a female this time, and resonates with the dominant image of machines and robots depicted as male creations in fiction and popular culture. Dixon suggests that "[t]he idea of anthropomorphic robots being a form of male procreation has been put forward by Jeff Cook, who describes a 'patriarchal dream of parthenogenesis' that escapes the 'the indeterminate and unreasonable realm' of flesh, nature, and the feminine. He reflects that there has been surprisingly little commentary on the notion of male procreation at play within developments in artificial intelligence, artificial life and robotics."[31] Therefore, the humanoid, who looks exactly like their dead son, can be seen as Hari's creation as he buys and assembles it, with a little help from his wife Max. We see him scene after scene adjusting and mending him, and most importantly he is the one who mostly controls Jån with the remote control. These all strengthen the idea that Hari performs the role of a male progenitor who aims perfection.

Their obsession with perfection is a dominant idea in the play and can be seen in their house, which looks like an IKEA catalogue, and also reveals itself in the rivalry and competition between Max and Hari and their friends Laurie and Paul. However, this obsession works at the cost of individuality and naturality, as conforming to these rules means standardization. The reference to the instruction manual underlines their attempt at achieving perfection (through faultless standardization). However, we also see them struggling with the manual, and unfortunately, the flatpack that is supposed to be sent in perfect condition, starts to show signs of imperfection very early on with the missing pieces:

> I paid for something perfect. I don't think it's too much to ask to be delivered something perfect. There are some missing components[...] Ball bearings, chrome, 5; Six pins,

---

29 Eccleshare, *Instructions for Correct Assembly*, 7.

30 Ibid., 8.

31 Steve Dixon, *Digital Performance: A History of New Media in Theater, Dance, Performance Art, and Installation* (Cambridge: The MIT Press, 2007), 291.

> stainless steel, 2; Circuit board, 1; Glass eye, grey-green, 1; Wig, Chestnut, 1; Toenails, 3, left big, right third, right pinky; Last one, lithium batteries.[32]

This customer complaint call made by Hari is another note on consumer society; however, it is also very important not only because this is the very first time the audience catches a glimpse of Dr Frankenstein's Monster, catching the phrases such as glass eye, wig, and toenails but at the same time makes it possible to see the humanoid as an assemblage: "All this, lines and measurable speeds, constitutes an *assemblage*[…] One side of a machinic assemblage faces the strata, which doubtless make it a kind of organism, or signifying totality, or determination attributable to a subject; it also has a side facing a *body without organs*, which is continually dismantling the organism, causing asignifying particles or pure intensities to pass or circulate[…]."[33] When assembled, Jån is just a plasticized body on the outside and works with a chip placed on the back of his head, which highlights and also comes as a criticism of Cartesian duality again. With this depiction of the pieces that make up his body, similar to the ideas proposed by Deleuze and Guattari, he becomes an assemblage, a "*body without organs*" as he is a machine assembled in a Garage. He will be "a kind of organism" as he will interact with humans and show signs of a capacity for change and adaptation as the play progresses. If we are to consider the bits and pieces that make up any organism, this view also leaves us with further questions concerning the status of Jån. As he is seen as a foster son or a body double of their dead son, there are the undertones of seeing it as a reflection of the "sacred" human body, with his body parts that look like "*the perfect plastic parts of a male manikin.*"[34] However, we see Hari using Jån's elbow as a paperweight[35] or he loses his belly button "again,"[36] and when these instances couple with the idea of the manikin, the sacredness of Jån's body parts are questioned, as they would not be similarly treating their son's body. Haraway challenges the idea of sacredness by saying that "[N]o objects, spaces, or bodies are sacred in themselves."[37] Thus, this approach pushes us to realize that the sacredness of the human body is a human construct, in this sense Jån's body parts are no different from human body parts.

---

32 Eccleshare, *Instructions for Correct Assembly*, 9.

33 Deleuze and Guattari, *A Thousand Plateaus*, 4.

34 Eccleshare, *Instructions for Correct Assembly*, 12.

35 Ibid., 27.

36 Ibid., 36.

37 Donna J. Haraway, *Simians, Cyborgs, and Women: The Reinvention of Nature* (New York: Routledge, 1991), 163.

However, there is always this parallelism between furniture pieces and the humanoid as Hari refers to the process as such: "It's all these separate parts. [...] You're looking at them and thinking okay this doesn't make any sense how will this ever fit together and be our new bed or desk or whatnot [...] but then two hours later once it's all come together you're looking at it and thinking wow."[38] Therefore, the humanoid's identity, function and definition vary, he turns into a hybrid character[39]: perfect like Man, yet also a pet, an object similar to a piece of furniture, and a technological toy. As I mentioned before, through a critical posthumanist spectacle, cyborgs, robots and hybrids are becoming a part of the marginalized others in our age, occupying an ambivalent place, thus the boundaries and the distinctions between organic beings and machines are being beclouded. Donna Haraway also discusses this idea by suggesting a "leaky distinction" between species. Contemplating on Haraway's ideas LePage indicates that "the cyborg finds form as 'three crucial boundar[ies]' are broken down, boundaries between the human and animal, the animal-human (organism) and machine, and the physical and nonphysical. [...] these boundaries are 'thoroughly breached', 'leaky', 'thoroughly ambiguous', and 'very imprecise.'"[40] Although Jån is not a cyborg, his status is not different from a cyborg, he is also surrounded by ambiguity and breaches traditional boundaries as suggested in Haraway's seminal work. What we encounter on stage, concerning his status, is this evolutionary and transitive existence of a machine that is a commodity, an "Oedipal animal" that "draws *them* to a narcissistic contemplation,"[41] a human replica or a body double, and a desiring-machine that aims at becoming human, all at once:

> Pre-cybernetic machines could be haunted[...] But basically machines were not self-moving, self-designing, autonomous. They could not achieve man's dream, only mock it. They were not man, an author to himself, but only a caricature of that masculinist reproductive dream. To think they were otherwise was paranoid. Now we are not so sure. Late twentieth-century machines have made thoroughly ambiguous the difference between natural and artificial, mind and body, self-developing and externally designed, and many other distinctions that used to apply to organisms and machines. Our machines are disturbingly lively, and we ourselves frighteningly inert.[42]

38 Eccleshare, *Instructions for Correct Assembly*, 8–9.

39 This hybridity resonates with the actor's hybridity, and in particular with the hybrid presence of the actor that plays both Nick and Jån.

40 LePage, "Beyond Character," 56.

41 Deleuze and Guattari, *A Thousand Plateaus*, 240. My italics.

42 Haraway, *Simians, Cyborgs, and Women*, 152.

Moving from Haraway's historicizing of the machine-human interaction and the evolution of machines, Jån can be seen as a character on the stage that reflects this evolution; he starts his existence as a flatpack humanoid and an object of male procreation and technophilia but evolves into a more ambiguous "organism" by making it impossible for the audience to decide if he is just programmed to act this way, if his chip is broken, or if he is becoming human. These choices underline both technophilia and technophobia on Max and Hari's (and the audience's) part.

The scenes where Hari tries to communicate with him reveal how the human approach to machines is egoistical and consumerist. Similar to Dr Frankenstein, Hari assembles tiny bits and pieces and fiddles with the circuits on Jån's head and in a sense creates him. When he does not respond to the questions, he feels frustrated[43] and gets very excited when Jån responds in a manner that is expected from him.[44] At first, he likes impressing Paul with his new technological toy and he is also amazed by the humanoid's capacity. However, he slowly builds resentment and anger towards his monster as it completely goes out of his control and finds the solution in deactivating him. It begins with Hari animating him for the first time in the garage in Scene 2:

JÅN *wakes up, enthusiastically.*

JÅN Don't tell me this is my room? Honey I love it! OMG it's literally perfect I'm like having a literal heart attack right now.[...]

MAX Maybe turn down the "opinionated" dial?[...]

HARI fiddles with something on the back of JÅN's head.[...]

JÅN Bitch what was you thinking? These walls are like puke coloured or some shit.[...]

HARI [...] Ah, I think I've found the Sassy guage. I'll just take it right down shall I?[...]

JÅN switches to a meekness bordering on psychopathic.[...]

HARI *makes another change and JÅN switches to a confident, polite, eighteen-year-old boy.*

JÅN Hi.

MAX That looks better[45]

They are excited to see that their humanoid is functioning; however, when it comes to his word choices and reactions, they are not satisfied until they hear what sounds perfect for them. Thus, Hari plays with Jån's head to adjust him to their liking. Although we understand that Jån comes with a chip that is programmed to enable the user/owner to switch from one mood/personality to

43 Eccleshare, *Instructions for Correct Assembly*, 12.

44 Ibid., 13.

45 Ibid., 23–24.

another, we also realize that he has a sensory capacity as he can see around himself and talk about his surroundings. This leaves us asking if he is an intelligent humanoid, but also proves that he will not be allowed to use his own opinions as he is a commodity. This obsession with adjusting him to their idea of perfection continues throughout the play:

JÅN (*Talking with his mouth open and full of food.*) I cleaned my room.
HARI Jån?
JÅN Sorry. (*Still open and still full of food.*) I cleaned my room thoroughly.
MAX and HARI look at each other. MAX nods. HARI takes out the remote and taps on it a few times. Beep!
MAX What did you do again Jån?
He swallows the food, but mumbles monosyllabically into his chest with his head down like a sulky teenager[…]
HARI fiddles with the remote again and nods at MAX.
MAX Jån?
JÅN now talks eagerly and clearly looking each of them in the eye in turn.
JÅN I cleaned my room from top to bottom, it took ages but was worth it as now I have everything just the way I like it.[...]
JÅN I had a sandwich of bread and cheese and swimming.[...]
JÅN Swimming swimming swimming swimming swimming.
HARI gets up and fiddles with the back of JAN's head. […] taps on the remote.
JÅN Then I watched some television. A comedy show about some hilarious poofs who
HARI taps the remote. Beep.
JÅN A comedy show about some hilarious queer
Beep.
JÅN About some hilarious gay
Beep.[...][46]

Their conversations turn into a process of beeping that comes as an imposition of good manners and political correctness. Hari uses the remote control to tune Jån up to the best form of behaviour and speech; however, as they are not easily satisfied, the beeping damages him and makes him sound like a broken record in a literal sense of the word. This scene shows that human beings are not happy even with machines and find them lacking as the human mind is considered superior to other beings. It also refers to the unrealistic expectations of people from their children, in this case, a reference to what Max and Hari expected from Nick. Their interaction with Jån and the way they beep his undesired actions/words reflect their relationship with Nick and their obsession with perfection.

46 Ibid., 28–29.

The image of Nick in the flashbacks focuses on his negative sides as a son who threw away his future by dropping out of school, becoming an addict, stealing from his parents' house,[47] and failing in his attempts to restart his life. However, these scenes also criticize Max and Hari's parenthood, how they were incapable of seeing their son as an individual and wanted to control him the way they control Jån. However, their experience with Jån, which in a sense is a repetition of what they had gone through with Nick, proves that life and even human-made machines are not controllable by human beings.

Looking at Jån, this idea of an uncontrollable machine resonates with Haraway's leaky distinction and ambiguity. Jån slowly breaches the boundaries of being a machine, and it gets more difficult to control him using the remote controller. First, Max and Hari give him Nick's room, ask him to call them Mom and Dad. This can be seen as the beginning of the beclouding of boundaries between machine and human. Then he starts understanding the hidden messages behind the speeches of Max and Hari, and he expresses these things they cannot. Hari praises Jån's memory by saying, "[I]f you want to tell it a story about yourself,[…] if you programme it right he'll remember all that stuff and upload it to the cloud[…]."[48] Although he is still being controlled by Hari or Max, and says whatever they want to hear, his words make the audience think about his capacity for intelligence, feeling and recalling (recorded) memories:

HARI looks at MAX, checking she's asleep. Beep.

JÅN I just feel like, having thought about everything that happened, you know with Nick that.[…]
Well if Max had just listened to you[…]
Then maybe I don't know maybe things would have turned out differently.[49]

Although Hari uses the remote control to direct the conversation to this subject, Jån is not repeating recorded sentences but probably derives them from the memories of previous conversations. The word "thought" specifically draws attention as it is suggestive of a thinking process. As Braidotti explains "[a]nother name for subjectivity, according to Guattari, is autopoietic subjectivation, or self-styling, and it accounts both for living organisms, humans as self-organizing systems, and also for inorganic matter, the machines. […] This results in a radical redefinition of machines as both intelligent and generative."[50] She also suggests

47 Ibid., 45.
48 Ibid., 16–17.
49 Ibid., 57.
50 Braidotti, *The Posthuman*, 94.

that "[m]achinic autopoiesis means that the technological is a site of post-anthropocentric becoming, or the threshold to many possible worlds."[51] Thus, Jån's transformation or improvement can be seen as a "machinic autopoiesis" and a promise of a "post-anthropocentric becoming," although he will face failure.

A similar conversation happens between Jån and Max, yet this time we realize that the conversation happens naturally, Jån becomes the voice of Max's bottled-up feelings concerning the bragging attitude of her friend Laurie, and the beeping is used for making Jån's sentences more graphic:

JÅN And what makes it worse is that silent judgement.
MAX reaches for the remote control. Beep. Pause.
What makes it worse is that smug little bitchy judgement face.[…]
sometimes I'd wish Nick had got Amy involved too then she'd
see.
Beep.[…]
Sometimes I'd wish Nick had gone out with Amy and that he'd fuck her stupid perfect little brains out.[52]

This conversation not only reveals Jån's gradual enhancement but also points out the problem of Max and Hari's unrealistic expectations, which start working on Jån, as well. As a desiring machine, he wants to be human, a desire that is triggered by Max and Hari's desire to make this humanoid their son for egotistical aims. He tries to achieve this by making "his parents" happy by becoming the reflection of their dreams and wishes. Dixon suggests that "Wiener [...] considered at length the humanization of machines, maintaining that the question of whether machines could be considered to be alive or not was largely semantic. For Wiener, machines were alive because they were physically animate and operationally active."[53] Jån is alive not only because he is animate and active, but also because he shows human characteristics, so he symbolizes the humanization of machines. However, the pressure of various expectations from him and not being able to fit into the definition of either the machine or the human lead to his breakdown. He asks if he must perform when he meets Laurie, Paul and Amy, which points out the fact that he has at least two selves that he is aware of: his private self and public self.

During dinner, after Laurie and Paul brag about Amy without even giving her the chance to talk for herself, Jån says that he is also "[t]trying to go to University"

---

51 Ibid., 94.
52 Eccleshare, *Instructions for Correct Assembly*, 58–59.
53 Dixon, *Digital Performance*, 277.

and his "real passion lies in management and hospitality."[54] Similar to Nick, and more importantly like Hari, he wants to start a café, and he would also "like to do a design subsid"[55] like his Mom. This dinner scene, along with a few other scenes, is a replica of a scene with Nick; Jån replaces Nick, and his plans come both as a desire to correct Nick's mistakes and impress Max and Hari's friends. Unfortunately, the dinner gradually gets tensed up as he says he visited a brothel and now dates Danika, "a prostitute"[56] then talks about his plans of having a "fried chicken place in front of every school in England" which means selling unhealthy food to kids just for profit.[57] The others are not comfortable with the things he is saying, finding it offensive, although he just reveals the hard facts concerning women trafficking and unhealthy food marketing. He is in a way found odd for speaking the truths they prefer blocking out and for being a robot that talks about these experiences. Realizing the tension, he says he "changed his mind"[58] and repeats his ideas in a politically correct way. However, he gets frantic and terrifies the group with his actions:

> *JÅN grabs AMY by the arm.* […]
> **JÅN** (*Dragging her to her feet.*) I want us to have children and be a happy family just like all of you guys.[...]
> *He pushes her down onto the table, standing over her, wrestling with her arms. The adults scream and stand, shocked. JÅN begins to pull at her skirt, fumble with his fly*[59]

Jån, actually reflects what the others see as the definition of a perfect life and tries to replicate it; "[l]ike a soul that seeks incarnation, like a piece of metal ignited by the divine force of electricity, the (female) robot is a potential life longing to be actualized."[60] Jån is not a female robot, but he is a "technological body-double"[61] that wishes to "be actualized." However, similar to Frankenstein's Monster, his request is denied, and after attempting to rape Amy, rather than impressing the others, he utterly terrifies them. Max and Hari are in a state of panic as he destroys each perfect room and cannot be controlled with the remote control anymore. Although these are significant signs of his hybridity, Jån becomes a

54 Eccleshare, *Instructions for Correct Assembly*, 70.
55 Ibid., 71.
56 Ibid., 71.
57 Ibid., 72–73.
58 Ibid., 73.
59 Ibid., 75–76.
60 Braidotti, *Metamorphoses*, 220.
61 Ibid., 220.

technological monster for all of them, the fear of the unknown takes the shape of technophobia, and this prepares Jån's end as he fails to be a machine or a human, at least in Max and Hari's terms.

As LePage discusses, "[r]obots, failing to be human – failing even to meet the standards of behaviour of the most, supposedly, 'inferior' kind of human: the 'savage' – are, here, deemed incapable of any kind of intention or thought."[62] Thus, although he cries and begs Hari to give him another chance, Hari disassembles his body parts and turns him off.[63] If we go back to the argument that Jån as a humanoid turns into a marginalized other, what happens to him is also a result of being a commodity. As Braidotti indicates "the bodies of the empirical subjects who signify difference (woman/native/earth or natural others) have become the disposable bodies of the global economy."[64] The assembling and disassembling of Jån and his taking his place among the marginalized others also resonate with Haraway's idea of being "feminized" which "means to be made extremely vulnerable; able to be disassembled, reassembled, exploited [...]."[65] As a nonhuman entity, Jån serves anthropocentric and consumerist purposes, he is, in a sense, assembled, feminized, and when he gets out of control he is disassembled. Jån turns into our futuristic other in an anthropocentric world and can be grouped with nonhuman animals and other marginalized beings. All of these raise important questions concerning the machine as an intelligent being with free will and a capacity for change, but more importantly, concerning the definition of a human/oid.

These boundaries are completely breached when Hari offers Max placing chips in their heads. They lose/kill their second son and are still not able to realize seeking perfection is an unrealistic aim. The problems they have gone through with Nick, which caused by their unrealistic expectations, although Nick challenges his father by saying "Nobody's perfect Dad,"[66] are repeated with their machinic son Jån, as well. However, Max and Hari, in both cases, are not able to see that it is not the external world that is faulty, but it is their obsession with perfection. As they are not able to stop expecting perfection and are tired of their thoughts, Hari, as if it is a mundane thing to do, offers to use chips that

62 LePage, "Beyond Character," 29.
63 Eccleshare, *Instructions for Correct Assembly*, 85
64 Braidotti, *The Posthuman*, 111.
65 Haraway, *Simians, Cyborgs, and Women*, 166.
66 Eccleshare, *Instructions for Correct Assembly*, 45.

would enable them to control their minds and bodies which will make them, as Max suggests, perfect:

HARI It wouldn't be that hard. The truth is most of this is just casing. In theory
there's no reason you couldn't[...]
Slide it in and hook it up
MAX Because I'm finding mine so messy.
HARI Me too.[...]
I wake up and I've just got so many[...]
Thoughts.[...]
Oh god I'd love
MAX A good night's sleep.[...]
The world can never be perfect that's not going to happen.[...]
But we can.[67]

Braidotti argues that "[t]he relationship between the human and the technological other has shifted in the contemporary context, to reach unprecedented degrees of intimacy and intrusion. The posthuman predicament is such as to force a displacement of the lines of demarcation between structural differences, or ontological categories, for instance between the organic and the inorganic, the born and the manufactured, flesh and metal, electronic circuits and organic nervous systems."[68] Hari, referring to the human body as a casing that can be slid and hooked with a chip that can easily be done through the use of a manual, becomes the epitome of intimacy and intrusion discussed by Braidotti.

As mentioned before, the play depicts the breaching of boundaries on many levels, beginning with the intimacy and humanization of a humanoid and ends with the mechanization of human beings. However, this breaching or the "displacement of the lines of demarcation" does not happen for embracing the other and coexisting peacefully. Max and Hari's process of becoming machine is not a Braidottian experience, it is physically and mentally *being* a machine. They are enhancing their minds, not only in the sense of making it better or perfect but also having the luxury/choice of turning one's thoughts and senses off. Hari hooks Jån's chip up his head, but when he realizes that the spare chip is soaked, he uses the chip of an old fax machine for Max, and they use the batteries of an electric toothbrush to activate the chips. It can be suggested that Hari continues with his male desire for technological procreation as well as his masculine superiority, as his chip is fancier than Max's. Nevertheless, they both end up with a

67 Ibid., 87.

68 Braidotti, *The Posthuman*, 90.

brain that works and controls the body like a simple domestic machine functioning with the batteries of a toothbrush. This experience is preferred to the organic functioning of the brain and the body that keeps track of personal and collective experiences. With the idea of controlling the brain with a chip which as a result uses the body only as a "casing" and (re)turns it into a "body without organs," they fall into the same old trap of Cartesian duality. By turning off the body's connection and interrelation to the mind and ignoring its functioning as an information gatherer, a knowing, feeling, and thinking entity they take us to Lyotard's discussion of a mind without a body: "The body might be considered the hardware of the complex technical device that is human thought. If this body is not properly functioning, the ever so complex operations, the meta-regulations to the third or fourth power, the controlled deregulations [...] are impossible. [...] In other words your philosophy is possible only because the material ensemble called 'man' is endowed with very sophisticated software."[69] It can be suggested that they are both shutting down the mind and the body rather than conforming to that duality, however, the only alteration is made to the brain, and the body is seen as an extension of it that will be controlled by the chip. After these small homemade operations, they open their eyes to a "new dawn."[70]

In the last scene of the play, we see Max and Hari in Nick's room, which is now turned into a gym, and they talk about how they keep hydrated and will be upgrading the gym with "yoga mats" and "a pull-up bar" while they are running "on treadmills."[71] When we come to the end of the play, with their transformation into cyborgs, half-human half-machine entities, they are able to accept the loss of their son and find the "perfection" they have been looking for. As Dixon argues "even the cult of the body as expressed in the late-twentieth-century desire for 'the body beautiful,' tailored through diet, gymnasium culture, cosmetics, and plastic surgery, is a Cartesian triumph of mind over matter."[72] The transformation of Nick's room into a gym and their new obsession with exercising can be read as the "cult of the body," the perfection they expected from the son is now directed towards their bodies.

69 Lyotard, *The Inhuman*, 13.
70 Eccleshare, *Instructions for Correct Assembly*, 89.
71 Ibid., 95.
72 Dixon, *Digital Performance*, 213.

Conclusion

Braidotti indicates that "[t]he metaphorical or analogue function that machinery fulfilled in modernity, as an anthropocentric device that imitated embodied human capacities, is replaced today by a more complex political economy that connects bodies to machines more intimately."[73] Therefore, Jå̲n as a humanoid assembled and used for anthropocentric purposes can be seen as a posthumanist criticism of transhumanism, as the main message that lies beneath his existence is the desire to control, change, and surpass the mortality of the body, defects of the mind, and the faults in behaviour as well as enslaving machines. To repeat my argument posed in the introduction, Jå̲n not only reflects the transhumanist desires for perfection but also represents humanity's new other that is in a sense exploited and abused for anthropocentric ends. Braidotti suggests that "the technological anthropomorphic machine is an object of imaginary projections and fantasy. [...] The automaton lends itself to such fantasmatic usages and it therefore plays a paradoxical role within scientific discourse."[74] Max and Hari project their own dreams and fears onto the humanoid, intending to prove themselves as good and capable parents who can raise their children to perfection. Jån is Nick's, and in a more general sense, humans' body double and exists as an anthropomorphic machine, but he is also beyond machine.

Eccleshare's deliberate choice of drawing a thin line between being a machine and being a human helps us investigate the waters of the posthuman condition while questioning the anthropocentric approach of humanity. The audience sees the faulty approaches to becoming machine and becoming human: On the one hand, Jån's attempt at becoming human fails because he dreams of being a human, and secondly, as a machine and the monstrous other, his becoming or being is not allowed. On the other hand, Max and Hari's attempt at becoming machine fails similarly, rather than an idea of becoming, they choose to turn into machines and turn off their human characteristics. They lack a critical approach that would make a peaceful co-existence possible.

This failure comes as a criticism of our unwillingness to "the creation of a new social nexus and new forms of social connection with these techno-others."[75] Thus, Eccleshare is able to call the audience's anthropocentricity into question by making them face their own prejudices and fears when it comes to nonhuman entities and transhumanist desires. As Braidotti suggests "[e]thically, we need

73 Braidotti, *The Posthuman*, 89–90.

74 Braidotti, *Metamorphoses*, 216.

75 Braidotti, *The Posthuman*, 103.

to re-locate compassion and care of both human and non-human others in this new frame,"[76] theatre as a form of storytelling can challenge human culture and help deconstruct our anthropocentricity through the use of these stories.

Bibliography

Bostrom, Nick. *The Transhumanist FAQ*. World Transhumanist Association, 2003. https://www.nickbostrom.com/views/transhumanist.pdf.

Braidotti, Rosi. *Metamorphoses: Towards a Material Theory of Becoming*. Cambridge: Polity Press, 2002.

Braidotti, Rosi. *The Posthuman*. Cambridge: Polity Press, 2013.

Colebrook, Claire. *Gilles Deleuze*. London: Routledge, 2002.

Davies, Tony. *Humanism*. London: Routledge, 1997.

Deleuze, Gilles and Felix Guattari. *Anti-Oedipus: Capitalism and Schizophrenia*. Minneapolis: Minneapolis University Press, 2000.

Deleuze, Gilles and Felix Guattari. *A Thousand Plateaus: Capitalism and Schizophrenia*. Minneapolis: Minneapolis University Press, 2005.

Descartes, René. "Discourse on Method." In *Discourse on Method and Meditations on First Philosophy*. Translated by Donald A. Cress, 1–33.Indianapolis: Hackett Publishing Company, 1998.

Dixon, Steve. *Digital Performance: A History of New Media in Theater, Dance, Performance Art, and Installation*. Cambridge: The MIT Press, 2007.

Eccleshare, Thomas. *Instructions for Correct Assembly*. London: Oberon Books Ltd., 2018.

Garreau, Joel. *Radical Evolution: The Promise and Peril of Enhancing Our Minds, Our Bodies and What It Means to Be Human*. New York: Broadway Books, 2005. Kindle.

Harway, Donna J. *Simians, Cyborgs, and Women: The Reinvention of Nature*. New York: Routhledge, 1991.

LePage, Louise Emma. "Beyond Character: A Post/Humanist Approach to Modern Theatre." PhD diss., Royal Holloway College, University of London, 2012. https://pure.royalholloway.ac.uk/portal/files/6385784/phd_thesis_louise_lepage.pdf.

Lyotard, Jean-François. *The Inhuman*. Translated by Geoffrey Bennington and Rachel Bowlby. Stanford: Stanford University Press, 1991.

76 Ibid., 110.

Pirie, Hamish and Thomas Eccleshare. "Instructions for Correct Assembly Flatpack Interview." Interview by Royal Court Theatre. March 2018. video. https://royalcourttheatre.com/whats-on/instructions/.

Sharon, Tamar. *Human Nature in an Age of Biotechnology: The Case for Mediated Posthumanism*. Dordrecht: Springer, 2014.

Taipale, Sakari, et al. "Introduction: Situating the Human in Social Robots." In *Social Robots from a Human Perspective*, edited by Jane Vincent et al., 1–7. Heidelberg: Springer, 2015.

Hakan Gültekin

Post-Neoliberalism, Free Market and Disillusionment:

Anders Lustgarten's *If You Don't Let Us Dream, We Won't Let You Sleep*

Introduction

This chapter sets out to explore the significance of post-neoliberalism in Anders Lustgarten's If *You Don't Let Us Dream, We Won't Let You Sleep* (2013). Acknowledging that any literary production cannot be examined without considering a bigger and more complex social structure, the study attempts to find out about the dialectical relationship between Lustgarten's play and the society in which the characters live. Anders Lustgarten is regarded in Britain as the most exciting political playwright of recent years. He won both The inaugural Harold Pinter Playwright's Award and The Catherine Johnson Award with the play this chapter examines. Lustgarten depicts society from the standpoint of corruption, decadence and hopelessness. His play *Lampedusa*, staged in 2015, mainly revolves around the migrant crisis. *A Day at the Racists* tells the story of betrayal to the working class in Britain.

Post-neoliberalism is a relational perspective on governance that emerged after the 2008 global financial crisis. Post-neoliberalism is also a concept given to a period on which a global climate crisis affected the whole world and vital resources were crudely consumed. Most importantly, the post-neoliberal era has been built on serious political disappointments fuelled by neoliberal policies. In the play set in a dystopian UK, the business representatives decide that the financially burdensome culture of addiction must be eliminated. For this purpose, the state invents "Unity Bonds," a tool that will generate returns if the number of people committing crimes to the investor or taking drug treatment drops to a certain level. Thus, the state wants to shift the cost of social repair to the private sector. The play takes place in a dystopian universe in which free market principles dominate every area of society, and the basic rights of citizens such as health, education and housing are commodified, the basic principle of neoliberalism, dominates every area of society, and the basic rights of citizens such as health, education and housing are commodified. Using close reading method, this study deals with the analysis of the interactive arrangements between the play and its socio-political context.

The impetus behind this study is to investigate the ways in which Anders Lustgarten critiques the post-neoliberal era which destroys the foundational values of the western society and the social consensus lying in its base by deepening the economic and social injustices.

From Neo to Post: Long Journey of Liberalism

This part of the chapter will outline the basic orientation of neoliberal policies, the development of the financial-centred accumulation process, and the crisis and post-crisis practices of this accumulation model. In the following part of the study, the policies that became apparent after the 2008 financial crisis, also known as the crisis of neoliberalism, and evaluated under the concept of post-neoliberalism, will be discussed. After the Second World War, the world had changed radically and pretensions of the Axis powers to organize continental Europe and East Asia had collapsed.[1] In this respect, the economic elites of the advanced capitalist world had to create a new alternative system in order to survive in postwar era.[2] Keynesian economics, advocating a mixed economy in which the private sector was predominant but the state and public sectors played a major role, became the basic economic theory of the post-war established order. The economic recession that started in the late 1960s prepared the conditions for the transition to a new paradigm in economic policies. A new approach has dominated economic policy practices, symbolizing a break from the Keynesian practices of the post-war period. Neoliberal policies, which allow the unimpeded flow of capital and claim that the free market can be a solution to all kinds of economic problems, has started to become widespread.

In *The SAGE Handbook of Neoliberalism*, the neoliberal approach is described as advocating unrestrained economic liberalization, complete privatization, and total marketization and it opposes any kind of interference or regulation by the state.[3] As David Harvey points out, since the beginning of the 1970s, it is observed that there was a sympathetic point of view to neoliberalism in the

1 Charles S Maier, "The politics of productivity: foundations of American international economic policy after World War II." *International organization* 31, no. 4 (1977): 608.

2 Hakan Gültekin, The Critique of Neoliberalism in David Hare's Plays. Çizgi Publishing, (2021), 15

3 Damien Cahill, et al., eds., The SAGE *Handbook* of *Neoliberalism* (London: Sage, 2018), 23.

political-economic practices and theories of the advanced capitalist countries.[4] Privatizations and deregulations made by the neoliberal state spread rapidly among the advanced capitalist countries and became the norm. Advanced capitalist countries quickly pioneered the establishment of a neoliberal world.

British Prime Minister Margaret Thatcher and United States President Ronald Reagan played important roles in neoliberalism being the only viable economic and political hegemonic ideology of the capitalist camp in the 1980s.

In the United States, Ronal Reagan implemented a thoroughly neoliberal economics program called Reaganomics. On the other side of the Atlantic, the British Prime Minister Margaret Thatcher also implemented an individualist economic program, positioned against the welfare state and collective mind. On the other hand, neoliberal economic principles began to be seen not only in the capitalist camp, but also in the other side of the cold war, the socialist bloc. As Chaohua Wang reports, The People's Republic of China, which met neoliberal principles in the 1970s, became the world's most dynamic economy in the 90s, surpassing Japan as the country to export the most goods to the USA.[5] The 90s, the golden age of Neoliberal policies in the Western camp, have been called "the roaring nineties." According to Anthony Giddens, adviser to British Prime Minister Tony Blair, who was in power from 1997 to 2007, the Labour Party needed to develop a new understanding, and this necessity led to party policies called "the Third way." The third way meant that the Labour Party abandoned traditional left values and compromised with neoliberalization. As Gultekin addresses, post-cold war social democracy did not have to make a choice between Keynesianism or Thatcherism, alternatively the Labour Party was able to build a third path by combining two dominant democratic approaches.[6] Tony Blair in the UK and Bill Clinton in the United States were key representatives of the second wave of neoliberalism, hoping to create a socially conscious market globalism. Unlike their predecessors, Blair and Clinton tried to synthesize the harsh rules of market globalism into a set of ethical concepts.

Neoliberalism, which emerged with the crisis of the Keynesian economic model in the 1970s, began to be associated with other crises in the 2000s. The new millennium began with the Republican Bush government's invasions of Afghanistan and Iraq, respectively, and these interventions led to serious

4 David Harvey, A Brief History of Neoliberalism (Oxford: Oxford University Press, 2007).

5 Chaohua Wang, ed., *One China, Many Paths*. (London: Verso, 2003).

6 Gültekin, The Critique of Neoliberalism in David Hare's Plays.

criticism of neoliberalism's argument that free markets would bring peace and tranquillity. On the other hand, the biggest and most important crisis of the new millennium is the 2008 global financial crisis. In the end of the first decade of the 2000s, a market crisis originating in the USA emerged and after the crisis that sharpened in 2008, the stability of finance-centred accumulation was tried to be restored with state interventions. After the 2008 crisis, the state's interventions in the market, which is claimed to be managed by an "invisible hand" in the neoliberal order, herald the end of neoliberalism and the beginning of a new era. This marks the beginning of the post-neoliberal era in economic and political circles. Post-neoliberalism presents a relational perspective on governmentality in the context of a post-global present of climate change, resource exhaustion, and disillusionment with neoliberal reforms.[7] After the 2008 Global Economic crisis, it became clear that neoliberalism fell short of preventing the contradictions posed by its own practices.

With the limits of crisis management in neoliberalism, different proposals and strategies have come to the fore. Different rules and strategies developed to overcome the crisis of neoliberal financial market capitalism have been discussed under the concept of post-neoliberalism. From this point of view, post-neoliberalism is both a set of rules, an ideological attitude, and the name given to an era. Post-neoliberalism always develops in an incomplete "hybrid" manner.[8] According to Yates and Bakker, post-neoliberalism is not a policy of abandoning neoliberalism altogether. It is a tendency to move away from certain aspects of neoliberal policy prescriptions. In particular, it aims to restructure the state power against free market regulation and to prevent the social concerns created by the market economy. It aims to revitalize citizenship through people's active participation to the governmental procedures.[9]

One of the most distinctive features of the post-neoliberal period is the criticism of the destruction brought by neoliberalism, which has been the dominant ideological formula of the world economy for nearly 40 years. In order to better understand post-neoliberalism, a clear definition of neoliberalism must first be made. As Steger and Roy defines, Neoliberalism is a doctrine that advocates the utopian project of a society organized around self-regulating markets and free

7 Patti Lather, "Updata: Post-Neoliberalism," Qualitative Inquiry 26, no. 7 (2020): 768.

8 Pierre Gautreau and Perrier Bruslé Laetitia, "Forest Management in Bolivia under Evo Morales: The Challenges of Post-neoliberalism," Political Geography 68 (2019): 121.

9 Julian S Yates and Karen Bakker. "Debating the 'Post-neoliberal Turn' in Latin America," Progress in Human Geography 38, no. 1 (2014): 62–90.

from political interference.[10] David Harvey states that neoliberalism consists of a variety of contemporary political practices that improve the conditions for capital accumulation, even if they contradict the philosophical doctrine that the omnipotence of the market is at the heart of these neoliberal practices. Also, neoliberalism is the manifestation of a particular social interest in restoring the power of an economic elite.[11]

Nicola Sekler claims that in the post-neoliberal period, projects, trends and scenarios were reproduced in different fields and efforts were made to reproduce the bourgeois capitalist hegemony.[12] As a result, tendencies within and outside of neoliberalism develop simultaneously and parallel to each other. In this sense, the post-neoliberal state, while advocating for the reformation of state interventions, still tries to ensure the continuity of free market practices. Or, although the state opens the results of neoliberal policies to discussion, it also makes intellectual attempts to legitimize neoliberalism. While seeking social reformation grounds after neoliberal destruction through post-neoliberal alternatives, it also displays authoritarian and militaristic tendencies. This study examines Anders Lustgarten's play by taking this definition of post-neoliberalism as a guide. The present study considers post-neoliberalism both as a period and as a set of economic and ideological rules. From this point of view, the study also discusses the post-neoliberal state practices in Lustgarten's play, as well as the scenes depicting the dissolution of social integrity peculiar to the post-neoliberal era.

Commodification of Daily Life: Lustgarten's Unity Bonds

Once post-neoliberalism is considered as a period, the destruction of neoliberalism, which has ideologically dominated the world economy for nearly 40 years, is able to be clearly observed. The post-neoliberal era can be described as a real hell into which people who think they have found peace in the false paradise of the neoliberal era fall into. Consistent with this depiction, Lustgarten's play features a character list that includes individuals from many different classes and various occupational groups. Most of the working-class names might be seen in the play's character list; and characters from different professions such as workers, administrators, civil servants, nurses and politicians stand out. The

10 Manfred Steger and Ravi K. Roy. *Neoliberalism: A Very Short Introduction* (Oxford: Oxford University Press), 2010.

11 David Harvey, The New Imperialism (Oxford: Oxford University Press), 2005.

12 Nicola Sekler, "Postneoliberalism from and as a Counter-Hegemonic Perspective," Development Dialogue (2009): 59–71.

diversity of characters on a sectoral basis created by Lustgarten and the large number of characters in the play provide an opportunity to more clearly observe the neoliberal destruction. Because by its very nature, neoliberalism aims to commodify everything and put every economic sector at the disposal of the free market. In this respect, the critical notions found in the play from different economic sectors strengthen the claim that Lustgarten's play is a representation of the post-neoliberal era.

The main critical issue that Lustgarten emphasizes in the play is the systematic collapse of the social security system of the United Kingdom. Lustgarten creates a fictional administrative system called "Unity Bonds" to symbolize this collapse:

> **Taylor** But what if there was a way to turn those burdens into opportunities? (Holds up papers) Unity Bonds. Unity Bonds transfer the costs of social repair from the taxpayer to the private sector at a healthy return. Problem families can now be monetised, at a profit to investors and no cost to the public.
> **McLean** It's an incentive structure. The fewer people receive treatment for the problems, and/or the greater the reduction in offences, the higher the returns.
> **Taylor** It really is a game-changing solution.
> They all subtly look at Asset-Smith. He leafs through the papers. Beat.[13]

In this scene, bureaucrats and politicians working in the Department of Home and Business Affairs are seen in a meeting. They talk about practices that can be applied to find solutions to social problems such as addiction culture, poverty and child labour, which have increased in society in recent years. The solution that the department found to these serious social problems is called as "Unity Bonds." The unity bond mechanism is a system in which social problems are handled with fiscal concepts such as risk, benefit-harm and profit. That is, the state has a system in which social problems can be resolved only on the condition that it brings economic profit. Taylor is glad that the sociological situation problem families have may be resolved at no cost to the government and in a way that can generate profits for investors. However, the solution of social problems that will not bring economic return is never discussed at the meeting.

At the same meeting, participants equate union bonds, which concern the living standards of thousands of economically and socially disadvantaged families, with Indian infrastructure stocks or Chinese mining stocks, which are standard investment tools. Seeing the lives of millions of people as construction

13 Anders Lustgarten. *If You Don't Let Us Dream, We Won't Let You Sleep* (London: A&C Black, 2013), 2.

and mining industry practices is first and foremost a humanitarian problem. However, this is normal for the participants:

> **Thacker** I've got no problem with monetising social behaviour. It's the principle the private prison system is based on. My concern is if we were saddled with the impossible cases, the hard nuts. What does that do to our profit margins?[14]

Thacker clearly states in this scene that he sees no barriers to the marketing of social behaviour. Thacker utters this expression, which can be found to be blood-chilling under normal conditions, with extraordinary ease on stage. Thacker merely delivers his view, because in the fictional post-neoliberal universe created by Lustgarten, everything is reduced to economic profit and a free market economy. In Keynesian economies, the social security practices that the state will provide equally to every citizen without expecting any gain have undergone a neoliberal transformation and are no longer seen as a social right.

In the same scene, the audience learns from Thacker that prisons have also been privatized. Privatization is the most basic tool of neoliberalism, which advocates the idea of putting everything under the control of the free market. However, the idea of privatizing the country's judicial system through mechanisms called Unity bonds did not even occur to Margaret Thatcher, one of the most famous practitioners of neoliberalism. Maclean explains how the Unity Bonds system works in the judicial mechanism with the following words: If the number of people who commit crimes or receive treatment for drug addiction goes down to a certain level, investors get a return.[15] As Maclean clearly states, if there is any reduction in crime, investors profit. However, if the crime rate does not fall, investors cannot profit either. The aim of lowering the social crime rate, which is normally considered a social issue and should be done without expecting any benefit, has turned into an investment tool in Lustgarten's post-neoliberal universe.

In another scene, a teenager named Ryan and a man with "Competitive Confinement Ltd" written on his jacket are seen in a prison cell. The man has some documents and the man questions Ryan based on them. It soon becomes clear that Ryan had participated in a peaceful demonstration and was holding placards with political slogans:

> **Man** If you plead guilty, bearing in mind the relatively minor nature of the crime, I'd see you getting a very short custodial sentence. Three months maybe.

---

14 Ibid., 5

15 Ibid., 6.

Ryan Fuck off! Three months –

Man In return for which we'd write you the most glowing reference you can imagine. After all, we have what our website calls a "commonality of interests." If you come back here after you get out, we don't get paid.
Beat as the boy gathers himself.

Ryan One more time, mate, yeah: they weren't mine.

Man Or you can put that claim to a judge. It's quite a hostile environment out there at the minute. They were in your hands when you were arrested, Ryan. (Beat.) You don't have to decide now. I'll see you again in the morning.
He gets up and starts to leave. He stops and puts his hand on the boy's shoulder.
One more thing. If you do take up our offer and I see you back in here, I will come to your cell one night when you are sleeping, and I will pour battery acid over your face. OK? (Beat.) There'll be someone along to take you upstairs in a few minutes.
He leaves. The boy stares into space. Blackout.[16]

In a normal legal system, the interrogation of a criminal suspect is conducted only by government officials with legal academic licence. The role of the state is undisputed here because it is a rule that the police, judges and prosecutors, who are state officials, must be impartial.

However, in Lustgarten's fictional post-neoliberal state, the principle of impartiality in law has clearly disappeared and legal inquiries are now made by companies, the sole representatives of capital. Possible inquiries by companies whose sole reason for existence is to gain economic interests will be exactly like this scene. On stage, there is a man who clearly has no legal training and who speaks to Ryan like a mobster. He is bargaining with Ryan about the crime he has committed, and this negotiation is not on a fair ground. The presumption of innocence, which is one of the most basic elements of universal law, has disappeared and Ryan is present in this scene not as an equal citizen with rights, but as a bargaining commodity.

This scene also exhibits another post-neoliberal trend. While in the average democracy it was not even a crime for Ryan to peacefully demonstrate and hold political banners, in the fictional post-neoliberal state of Lustgarten it has become a crime requiring 3 months in prison. Lustgarten's fictional government is seriously authoritarian, and as Mitchell and Fazi clearly states, it is the reflection of the authoritarianism and centralization trend, which are important features of the post-neoliberal era. Neoliberalism, which has been advocating for years to shrink the state in all areas and to carry out state affairs at the maximum

16 Ibid., 30.

level by private companies, created the 2008 crisis.[17] As in every crisis period, this crisis period also brought nationalist politicians with authoritarian tendencies to the fore.

Donald Trump's election as president in the USA and UKIP's becoming the third party in the UK's general elections may be counted as examples of authoritarianism's sudden rise in politics.

Another area that gets its share of Lustgarten's critical approach in the play is the national health system of the United Kingdom. Scene 4 opens with Joan's dialogue with a nurse at a hospital. Joan desperately asks the nurse for help, but the nurse brings her some documents to fill out and sign. Although her health condition is urgent, no one takes care of her. Then a hospital manager arrives with documents and tells Joan "I'm afraid we can't make provision for you at this hospital, Joan."[18] Joan insists her condition is urgent and even mentions the name of her illness.

Administrator We can't make provision for you.
Joan Why not?
Beat.
Administrator Unity rejected your application.
Joan I didn't make an application. I didn't make an "application."
Administrator I'm very sorry, Joan. Please accept my sincere –
Joan Why'd they turn me down?
Administrator I couldn't say, it's a matter of commercial – [19]

Neoliberalism regards education, health and social security areas, which are seen as a citizenship right in the Keynesian understanding of capitalism, as a burden to the state and aims to bring these areas under the control of the free market economy through privatizations. To this end, neoliberal governments have over the years privatized all the mechanisms of the health sector, turning human health from being a universal social right into a property that can be bought and sold. Such capital-centred practices originating from neoliberalism have created serious social inequalities in access to health services. The period when these inequalities are most visible is the post-neoliberal period that emerged after the 2008 global economic crisis.

17 Mitchell William, and Thomas Fazi. *Reclaiming the State* (Chicago: University of Chicago Press Economics Books, 2017).
18 Lustgarten, *If You Don't Let Us Dream*, 35.
19 Ibid.,36.

Lustgarten draws attention to the neoliberal-related problems of the post-neoliberal period through the incident of the character named Joan. At the end of the scene, Joan doesn't get the health care she wants.

Another man, who is behind her in line and has no problem with his Unity Bonds information, gets ahead of her and gets medical care. In this way, Lustgarten emphasizes the inequality of health services and the hypocrisy of the health sector.

Conclusive Remarks: Post-Neoliberalism as a Neoliberal Dystopia

In *the Guardian*, Michael Billington laments the lack of political drama in recent years, describing Lustgarten's *If You Don't Let Us Dream, We Won't Let You Sleep* as "a polemical bombshell," noting that he has welcomed the play's arrival.[20] To Chris Megson, Lustgarten's drama places social and political issues centre stage, ranging from the housing crisis and the electoral ascendancy of far-right parties to the alienation of the urban working class and the racist scapegoating of immigrants.[21] Anders Lustgarten is described as a political dramatist, who believes that the society in which he lives must undergo radical change, a revolutionary transformation. From this point of view, Lustgarten mirrors contemporary British society, but this mirror is a broken mirror prepared with a Brechtian hammer, aiming to change reality.

Populism, political extremism and racism emerged as the three main outcomes of the post-neoliberal era. With the 2008 global financial crisis, populism and extremism began to gain strength in the United Kingdom, and especially in England, the central country of the kingdom, as in many other countries of the world. For example, the United Kingdom Independence Party (UKIP), which was founded in 1993 and was not even mentioned in the mainstream media for many years, showed a serious rise after the 2008 crisis. UKIP, which advocated Britain's separation from the European Union, thought that immigrants were destroying the country, and developed rhetoric that sometimes escaped racism, increased its vote rate to 12% in the 2015 general elections, while circulating around 2% of the votes for years. While this rise alone may be an indication of

20 Michael Billington, "If You Don't Let Us Dream, We Won't Let You Sleep" – Review. *The Guardian* (2013).

21 Chris Megson, "Can I Tell You About It?": England, Austerity and "Radical Optimism" in the Theatre of Anders Lustgarten," Journal of Contemporary Drama in English, 6, no. 1 (2018): 41–42.

the rise of populism in British mainstream politics, the fact that UKIP is one of the components of the winning side of the Brexit referendum strengthens this thesis.

While these were happening in Britain in the post-neoliberal period, interesting developments were also taking place on the opposite shore of the Atlantic. Businessman Donald Trump, generally known as a contractor, TV star and a tabloid figure in American history, was elected president of the United States in 2016, the same year as the Brexit referendum.

As if he had no share in the crisis due to his great wealth and the capitalist class he represents, Trump has built his entire election campaign on the consequences of the crisis. With all the post-neoliberal era brought, Trump appeared before the voters, made an accounting of neoliberalism and made countless promises to the American people. Trump came to power with populist rhetoric that scratched the public's sensitive points, such as building a wall on the Mexican border, deporting fugitives, or recalling American firms abroad. In the play, Jason's harassment of a Black employee in a bar because of his skin colour can be interpreted as Lustgarten's drawing attention to the increasing racism in the post-neoliberal era.

The Conservative Cameron government, which could not respond to the needs of the British people, especially the lower and middle classes, who were deeply affected by the 2008 financial crisis, failed in this sense. Indicators such as economic recession, foreign trade deficit, impoverishment of the middle class, unemployment and injustice in income distribution are among the economic realities of the Cameron period. Cameron's economic administration has created a serious disappointment in the British public. This growing disillusionment underlies the successful Brexit campaign. Under the Brexit campaign led by UKIP, this crisis, which has serious economic reasons and has almost become a social trauma, has distorted and created unrealistic economic discourses. For example, he claimed that the United Kingdom was taken over by foreign powers and conducted political campaigns with the theme of "take back our country." Making a social trauma political material instead of saying something new is an example of populism.

Post-neoliberalism is a set of ideals that somehow transforms neoliberalism, but is simultaneously characterized by economic policies embodied by the Washington Consensus. While there is scholarly debate about the defining features of post-neoliberalism, it is often associated with economic policies of nationalization and wealth redistribution, opposition to deregulation, financialization, free trade and the weakening of labour relations, and more generally with eco-finance. After the 2008 global financial crisis, there have been indications that there will be a major paradigm shift in the ideas and policies that guide national economies and global capitalism. While both left and right movements challenge the dominance of unelected technocrats and global markets, the populist policies of the following years appear as another outcome of post-neoliberalism.

Anders Lustgarten uses in his play not only the landscapes of economic depression that have had an impact in the post-neoliberal era but also situations that document post-neoliberal governance principles such as the rise of authoritarianism and financial centralization.

The death of social security and retirement comes at the beginning of the most obvious economic depressions of the post-neoliberal era and has taken its place in Lustgarten's narrative. The failure of the national health system in connection with the destruction of the social insurance system is another topic of Lustgarten's narrative of post-neoliberal devastation. In addition to these two major issues that hurt people in the real world, Lustgarten creates a fictional official judicial system and creates a fictional universe where people are judged based on their performance in the economic system called unity bonds. In *If You Don't Let Us Dream, We Won't Let You Sleep*, in which Lustgarten combines real world data and fictional systems, he leaves a warning for the future in this way: Neoliberalism is not dead; it is still living in its own hell.

Bibliography

Billington, Michael. "If You Don't Let Us Dream, We Won't Let You Sleep – Review." *The Guardian*, 2013. https://www.theguardian.com/stage/2013/feb/21/if-you-dont-let-us-dream-review.

Cahill, Damien, et al., eds. *The SAGE Handbook of Neoliberalism*. London: Sage, 2018.

Gautreau, Pierre, and Laetitia Perrier Bruslé. "Forest Management in Bolivia under Evo Morales: The Challenges of Post-neoliberalism." *Political Geography*, 68 (2019): 110–121.

Giddens, Anthony. *The Third Way: The Renewal of Social Democracy*. Hoboken, NJ: Wiley, 1999.

Gültekin, Hakan. *The Critique of Neoliberalism in David Hare's Plays*. Çizgi Publishing, 2018.

Harvey, David. *The New Imperialism*. Oxford: Oxford University Press , 2005.

Harvey, David. *A Brief History of Neoliberalism*. Oxford: Oxford University Press, 2007.

Lather, Patti. "Updata: Post-Neoliberalism." *Qualitative Inquiry* 26, no. 7 (2020): 768–770.

Lustgarten, Anders. *If You Don't Let Us Dream, We Won't Let You Sleep.* London: A&C Black, 2013.

Lustgarten, Anders. *Lampedusa.* London: Bloomsbury Publishing, 2015.

Lustgarten, Anders. *A Day at the Racists.* London: A&C Black, 2010.

Maier, Charles S. "The Politics of Productivity: Foundations of American International Economic Policy after World War II." *International Organization* 31, no. 4 (1977): 607–633.

Mitchell, William, and Thomas Fazi. "Reclaiming the state." Chicago: University of Chicago Press Economics Books, 2017.

Megson, Chris. "Can I Tell You About It?": England, Austerity and "Radical Optimism" in the Theatre of Anders Lustgarten. *Journal of Contemporary Drama in English*, 6, no. 1 (2018): 40–54.

Sekler, Nicola. "Postneoliberalism from and as a Counter-hegemonic Perspective." *Development Dialogue* 51 (2009): 59–71.

Steger, Manfred B., and Ravi K. Roy. Neoliberalism: A Very Short Introduction. Vol. 222. Oxford: Oxford University Press, 2010.

Wang, Chaohua, ed. *One China, Many Paths.* London: Verso, 2003.

Yates, Julian S., and Karen Bakker. "Debating the 'Post-neoliberal turn' in Latin America." *Progress in Human Geography* 38, no: 1 (2014): 62–90.

Pelin Doğan

"An International Crossroads of Female Pain"[1]

Intersectional Feminism: Jackie Kay's *Chiaroscuro*

Introduction

In the age of post-theories for over the past two decades, debates and researches pondering on the possibilities of pluralism in the social sciences have come to the fore. In his article titled "The New Cultural Politics of Difference," Cornel West propounds that this significant transformation emerging at the turn of the century established the engagement with "the new cultural politics of difference as a prerequisite for critics and artists."[2] West further points out that the salient features of this politics are "to trash the monolithic and homogeneous in the name of diversity, multiplicity and heterogeneity; to reject the abstract, general and universal in light of the concrete, specific and particular; and to historicize, contextualize and pluralize by highlighting the contingent, provisional, variable, tentative, shifting and changing."[3] Against this theoretical backdrop, unlike liberal or modernist conceptualization of identity, which assumes a universal, coherent and solid essence, the post-structuralist view of identity positions the individual into the intricately woven networks and practices of culture as well as prevailing discourses. In this context, as a multifaceted, dynamic and fluid phenomenon, identity is discursively and relationally constituted through varying interlocking and mutually constructing intersections. We can pursue the traces of these broader theoretical dynamics in the intersectional feminist discourse, which establishes a critical line against the hegemony of Western feminism concentrating on the experiences and interests of White and middle-class women

---

1 Referring to the different forms of women's subordination and exploitation in the social structures, Aleks Sierz calls Britain as "an international crossroads of female pain." Aleks Sierz, Rewriting the Nation: British Theatre Today (London: Methuen, 2011), 120.

2 Cornel West, "The New Cultural Politics of Difference," in The Postmodern Turn: New Perspectives on Social Theory, edited by Steven Seidman (Cambridge: Cambridge University Press, 1994), 65.

3 Ibid., 65.

as its subjects.[4] Coinciding with the third wave feminism, in the early 1990s, intersectional theory flourished to expose and dismantle exclusionary practices pushing women of colour to the periphery.

Over the last two decades, intersectionality has become a central issue in the feminist lexicon as well as gender studies and has taken on a transdisciplinary characteristic. The concept principally rejects the idea of homogeneous construction of the subject through a single axis of identity. Instead, it suggests a heterogeneous identity formation in which different categories of belonging overlap. In other words, in order to understand the constitution of a subject more comprehensively and in-depth, multiple identity belongings and relational dynamics should be taken into consideration. Only this perspective can reveal hierarchical social structures and power relations that encompass human words and actions. It is also significant to evaluate the individual experience, which manifests at the intersection of different axes of identity in the constitution of the subject. Indeed, a Black woman is not only discriminated on the grounds of blackness or womanhood separately but also exposed to various forms of domination and discrimination at the intersection of blackness and womanhood. However, a bourgeois Black woman does not experience discrimination in the same way as a lower-class Black woman would do. Even though a White female worker has an ethnically advantageous position, she may also be subject to class and sexist discrimination. Noticeably, domination and discrimination practices deepen with the intersection of different social and political categories such as class, race, and gender as the most common ones.[5]

Within the framework of the intersectional feminist approach, this chapter aims to explore the ways in which different identity categories overlap one another with special attention to Jackie Kay's play *Chiaroscuro* (1986). The play particularly revolves around the stories of four women coming from sexually, ethnically and politically diverse backgrounds. Starting with their names, they set off digging into their personal and cultural memories informed by migration, diaspora, hybridity, exploitation, and sexuality. The four women's quest for

---

4 Patricia Hill Collins, *Black Feminist Thought: Knowledge, Consciousness, and the Politics of Empowerment* (New York and London: Routledge, 2000), vii.

5 For further discussion, see Jennifer C. Nash, "Rethinking Intersectionality," *Feminist Review*, 89, no. 1 (2008); Vrushali Patil, "From Patriarchy to Intersectionality: A Transnational Feminist Assessment of How Far We've Really Come," Signs 38, no. 4 (2013); Nira Yuval-Davis, "What is Transversal Politics," *Soundings*, no. 12 (1999) and Nira Yuval-Davis, "Intersectionality and Feminist Politics," *European Journal of Women's Studies*, no. 13 (2006).

reasserting their identities and self-definition in the play poses the necessity to recognize their position at the crossroads of multiple axes of belonging in order to expose the different forms of domination and discrimination.

Intersectionality as an Analytical Tool

Coined by legal scholar and feminist Kimberlé Crenshaw in 1989,[6] the concept of intersectionality was introduced to the feminist theory by Black feminists including bell hooks (Gloria Jean Watkins) and Patricia Hill Collins as a response to the perceived failures of the mainstream discourse of the Western feminism. Crenshaw builds her concept on a concrete case. In 1976, Emma Degraffenreid and a group of Black female workers sued General Motors, an American multinational auto company, for racial and gender discrimination against employing women. The judge rejected the case on the grounds that the firm employed both Black and female employees. However, all the blacks employed in maintenance and industrial jobs were men, and women employed in secretarial and office jobs were all White. In this case, it seems that the legal discourse overlooked the exclusion suffered by Degraffenreid and other Black women.[7] Consequently,

6 Although it was conceptualized by Crenshaw, it had a long legacy in the history of Black feminism. It dates back to the 1960s and 1970s when "African-American women activists confronted the puzzle of how their needs simply fell through the cracks of anti-racist social movements, feminism, and unions organizing for workers' rights … Black women's specific issues remained subordinated within each movement because no social movement by itself would, nor could, address the entirety of discriminations they faced" (Collins and Bilge, 2020, 3). Before Crenshaw, other Black feminists also pointed at the multidimensionality of discrimination and practices of domination against Black women. This situation was called "multiple jeopardy" (1988, 47) by Deborah King, "double jeopardy" (1970) by Frances Beal, and "discrimination-within-discrimination" (1987–1988, 413) by Verna Kirkness. The issue was also resonated in Black feminist, activist, and academic Angela Davis's *Women, Race and Class* (1981) and Black lesbian feminist and activist Audre Lorde's *Sister Outsider* (1984). More strikingly, in 1851 Sojourner Truth gave a speech showing that the general assumption of womanhood and the reality of Black women did not compromise and asked the unsettling question: "Ain't I a Woman?" (1851). Many date the beginning of "intersectional thinking" to this speech given by Truth (Yuval-Davis 2011, 4).

7 Kimberlé Crenshaw, "The Urgency of Intersectionality," *TEDWomen* (2016), https://www.ted.com/talks/kimberle_crenshaw_the_urgency_of_intersectionality?language=en#t-294596

Black women's experience disappears as overlapping injustices to which they are exposed go unrecognized.[8]

In her article titled "Intersectionality Right Now!" Crenshaw offers a critical perspective with intersectionality, which she defines as "an analytical sensibility" and "a way of thinking about identities and their relation to power."[9] Concentrating on overlapping and mutually constructing forms of discrimination and exploitation to which Black women are exposed, she establishes an analogy with the intersections of the roads where racist and sexist discrimination intersect and traffic:

> Consider an analogy to traffic in an intersection, coming and going in all four directions. Discrimination, like traffic through an intersection, may flow in one direction, and it may flow in another. If an accident happens in an intersection, it can be caused by cars travelling from any number of directions and, sometimes, from all of them. Similarly, if a Black woman is harmed because she is in an intersection, her injury could result from sex discrimination or race discrimination [...] But it is not always easy to reconstruct an accident: Sometimes the skid marks and the injuries simply indicate that they occurred simultaneously, frustrating efforts to determine which driver caused the harm.[10]

A single-axis analysis of Black women's experiences that handle gender and race separately cannot provide a truly comprehensive understanding of their predicament. In her critique of one-dimensional exploration of social inequalities, Crenshaw states that different and intertwined modes of oppression materialize at the intersection of these identity belongings.[11] Thus, the compartmentalization of identity belongings renders Black women invisible.

Black feminists based their critique of Western feminism mainly on two issues: "The need to recognize the differences among women and the need to focus on the inclusive possibilities of feminism against its exclusionary character."[12] Angela Davis argues that this struggle is against the universalizing and

---

8 Crenshaw, "Demarginalizing the Intersection of Race and Sex: A Black Feminist Critique of Antidiscrimination Doctrine, Feminist Theory and Antiracist Politics," *University of Chicago Legal Forum* 1989, article 8 (1989): 141–143, https://chicagounbound.uchicago.edu/uclf/vol1989/iss1/8

9 Crenshaw, "Kesişimsellik Hemen Şimdi!" *5 Harfliler* (2017), http://www.5harfliler.com/kesisimsellik-hemen-simdi/

10 Crenshaw, "Demarginalizing," 149.

11 Crenshaw, "Mapping the Margins: Intersectionality, Identity Politics, and Violence against Women of Color," Stanford Law Review 43, no. 6 (1991): 1244.

12 Kathy Davis, "Intersectionality as Buzzword: A Sociology of Science Perspective on What Makes a Feminist Theory Successful," *Feminist Theory* 9, no. 1 (2008): 67–68.

exclusionary perception of the issue "as if all feminists were White and all blacks were male."[13] When talking about the struggle or suffering of the Black people, the Black male is in the foreground and Black woman's "Black" identity takes precedence over "woman" identity. Similarly, it seems that feminism's homogenizing category of "women" is not inclusive as regards the Black women's experience. However, the practices of discrimination faced by Black and White women are not the same because other intersecting identity categories transform the face and intensity of discrimination. For this reason, Black women, who are pushed to the periphery of both hegemonic spheres (race and gender) and suffer from both, focused on the Black women's experience that appears at the intersection of intricate power relations in order to articulate and make visible their particular experience. In her work titled *Black Feminist Thought*, Collins describes the complicated mechanisms of power with the concept of "the matrix of domination."[14] Accordingly, "[r]egardless of the particular intersections involved, structural, disciplinary, hegemonic, and interpersonal domains of power reappear across quite different forms of oppression."[15] Thus, intersectionality promises to reveal these complex power relations in order to bring the under-examined or unrecognized situations to the fore.

Black feminists argue that the second-wave feminism, due to its normative and exclusionary character, fails to recognize the diverse needs of women and the multiple forms of discrimination they are subjected to. Western feminism's homogenous understanding of women's oppression, interests and experience generate serious blind spots in the feminist theory by ignoring the practices of discrimination arising from the differences among women. They further assert that only gender-based or only race-based evaluation of a case will fall short of understanding their combination in the case of a woman of colour. Indeed, different social identity categories overlap and produce unique forms of discrimination. However, the mainstream feminist discourse that prioritizes the Eurocentric, White, middle-class women's experience and needs, leaves out the experience of women of colour and renders it invisible. The assumption of a universal category of women is constructed upon the ignorance of differences.

13 Angela Davis, "The Personal is Political: Gendered Identities in the Twenty-First Century," The Eight Biennial Associated Colleges of the South Gender Studies Conference, Rhodes College and the Gender and Sexuality Studies Department, 6–7 Mart 2009: 59.

14 Patricia Hill Collins, *Black Sexual Politics: African Americans, Gender, and the New Racism* (New York: Routledge, 2004), 18.

15 Ibid., 18.

Black feminists' challenge against the exclusionary character of Eurocentric feminism was also strengthened by the works of queer theorists like Judith Butler and postcolonial feminists like Chandra Talpade Mohanty. Thus, the scope of the intersectional theory extended to describe how interrelated power mechanisms subordinate the marginalized people such as LGBTI+ individuals, women of colour, lower-class women, disabled individuals and female refugees/asylum seekers. As Butler puts, "the insistence upon the coherence and unity of the category of women has effectively refused the multiplicity of cultural, social, and political intersections in which the concrete array of 'women' is constructed."[16] The intersectional theory seeks to give voice to the unique experiences of the individuals who are positioned as the outsiders of socially constructed norms. Pointing at the ubiquitous existence of gender hierarchy and struggle in every field of social life, Nancy Fraser writes:

> Each therefore requires feminist theorization. Each, however, is also traversed by other, intersecting axes of stratification and power, including class, "race"/ethnicity, sexuality, nationality, and age – a fact that vastly complicates the feminist project. Although gender dominance is ubiquitous, in sum, it takes different forms at different junctures and sites, and its character varies for differently situated women. Its shape cannot be read off from one site or one group and extrapolated to all the rest.[17]

Drawing upon Fraser's insights, it seems that one-dimensional identity politics falls short of articulating and analyzing the interconnected nature of the overlapping social identities in its entirety. An intersectional approach should be developed to recognize differences and privileges as an alternative model and analytical tool particularly within the contemporary socio-political circumstances of multicultural societies. It offers practical and theoretical policies for the recognition, enunciation and prevention of visible or invisible injustices, inequalities and privileges in order to explore diverse forms of otherization and subordination informed by multiple axes of social, cultural, political and economic divisions and belongings. In doing so, it can also shed light on the complexity of the dynamic and multivalent processes and operations of power relations.

The concept has been cherished as a significant contribution that Women's Studies have made.[18] Kathy Davis also praises intersectionality as it responds

16 Judith Butler, Gender Trouble: Feminism and the Subversion of Identity (London: Routledge, 1999), 19–20.

17 Nancy Fraser, "Pragmatism, Feminism, and the Linguistic Turn," in Feminist Contentions: A Philosophical Exchange (New York and London: Routledge, 1995), 159.

18 Leslie McCall, "The Complexity of Intersectionality," Signs 30, no. 3 (2005): 1771.

to "the most pressing problem facing contemporary feminism – the long and painful legacy of its exclusions."[19] Intersectionality makes diverse and overlapping forms and practices of discrimination visible and therefore it deciphers the operations of intricately woven power mechanisms. As Sigle-Rushton points out, "[t]hese concerns also resonate with postmodern and poststructuralist arguments that the act of categorization itself is part of the workings of power, producing, policing and stratifying subjects."[20] As an act of regulating and castigating differences, categorization involves the exertion of power. However, the social markers of identity act dynamically, fluidly and flexibly within the particular historical contexts and so deconstruct categories. Furthermore, as a "critical tool"[21] or "research methodology," intersectionality focuses on "the minority culture" to trace "how certain people seem to get positioned as not only different but also troublesome and, in some instances, marginalized."[22] In doing so, intersectionality opens up a discursive space for critical dialogue by raising upsetting questions and thus develops a way to "resist oppression, both its practices and the ideas that justify it."[23]

Jackie Kay's *Chiaroscuro*

The Scots Makar (2016–) Jackie Kay is a multifaceted author who produced poetry, short story, novel, children's literature, theatre plays and memoirs. In her work, the question of identity politics has been a major preoccupation, which largely relies upon Kay's own complex racial, cultural and societal ties. Born to a Nigerian father and a Scottish mother in 1961, Kay was adopted by a working-class Scottish couple as a baby. Being a writer of mixed-race descent who "speaks with a Glaswegian accent" and being a lesbian who defies the heteronormative dictates on sexuality, she is situated at the crossroads of multi-layered identity

19 Davis, "Intersectionality as Buzzword," 70.

20 Wendy Sigle-Rushton and Elin Lindström. "Intersectionality," *LSE Research Online* (2018): 5, http://eprints.lse.ac.uk/id/eprint/86427.

21 Ibid., 5.

22 Dorthe Staunæs, "Where Have All the Subjects gone? Bringing Together the Concepts of Intersectionality and Subjectification," NORA – Nordic Journal of Feminist and Gender Research 11, no. 2 (2003): 101.

23 Anna Carastathis, "The Concept of Intersectionality in Feminist Theory," Philosophy Compass 9, no. 5 (2014): 307.

belongings.[24] Hilariously pointing at her position of liminality, Kay states "I still have Scottish people asking me where I'm from. They won't actually hear my voice, because they're too busy seeing my face."[25] Drawing upon her own processes of identity formation, Kay states that identity is "something that's fluid, it's not something that's static and fixed" and explores its fluidity and multifaceted nature in her work.[26]

Commissioned by Theatre of Black Women, Jackie Kay's *Chiaroscuro* was first put on stage at the Soho Poly, London, on 19 March 1986.[27] Thirty-three years later in 2019, Lynette Linton, the artistic director of the Bush Theatre, revived the play whose concern still matters, apparently.[28] The play revolves around four women (Aisha, Yomi, Beth and Opal) coming from diverse backgrounds including Black, Asian descent, mixed-race, lesbian identities and their exploration of self-definition through reasserting their names, cultural history and identity belongings. Throughout the play, they dig into the depths of memory to "find a precise beginning" which is yet, quite "tough."[29] The search for identity in the play demonstrates that Black female identity is both influenced by and intertwined with different axes of belonging such as race, gender, sexual orientation and politics that often conflict with one another.

The play opens with four women telling the story of their names. Aisha is named after her grandmother on her mother's side, who was born in the Himalayas. Her parents came from Asia to the UK "in 1953 to work and save and work and one day return home."[30] Although they were initially "invited guests," later on, they were "treated like gatecrashers."[31] Yomi who was born in Nigeria and called after her mute grandmother finally ends up in Britain as a

24 C. L. Innes, "Accent and Identity: Women Poets of Many Parts," in *Contemporary British Poetry: Essays in Theory and Criticism*, edited by James Acheson and Romana Huk (New York: State University of New York Press, 1996), 335.

25 Libby Brooks, "Don't tell me who I am," *The Guardian*, 12 January 2002, https://www.theguardian.com/books/2002/jan/12/fiction.features

26 Jackie Kay, "An interview with Jackie Kay," *The Children's Poetry Archive*, 2005, https://childrens.poetryarchive.org/interviews/an-interview-with-jackie-kay/

27 Jackie Kay, *Chiaroscuro*, in *The Methuen Drama Book of Plays by Black British Writers*, (London: Bloomsbury, 2011), 61.

28 Michael Billington, "*Chiaroscuro* Review – Jackie Kay's Play is More Gig than Theatre," *The Guardian*, 2019, https://www.theguardian.com/stage/2019/sep/09/chiaroscuro-review-jackie-kay-theatre-bush-lynette-linton

29 Kay, *Chiaroscuro*, 63.

30 Ibid., 71.

31 Ibid., 71.

single mother. Her grandmother tells stories through drawing and painting to the children. Beth is called after her great-great-great-great grandmother on her father's side "who was taken from Africa to slavery in America and raped often; who had children that were each taken from her."[32] Beth further states that her father "called [her] Beth because [her] grandmother's African name was whipped out of her: This was the name the White people gave her with welts in her Black skin. He said that history had to be remembered too."[33] Beth's father is from St. Vincent in the Caribbean and her mother is a White English woman. Opal, who is a Black woman of mixed race, comes of unknown parentage and as there is no family name to be passed down, she is named after a stone. She does not remember her parents and describes how she waited for "foster parents" who "never arrived."[34] While Aisha and Yomi have a shared experience of immigration, Opal and Beth are of mixed-race, lesbians and born in Britain. As the title of the play *Chiaroscuro*[35] and the organization of the stage chiefly in grey and Black colours might implicate these four Black women undergo the processes of confrontation and reconciliation with their personal and, in a broader sense, cultural memory/history, through their multiple forms of racial and sexual belonging both within inter- and intra-communal contexts. The constant interplay of light and shadow on the stage also signifies that identity is in a relentless flux of becoming due to the processes of folding and unfolding personal/cultural heritage within the particularities of time and space. In her postscript to the play, Kay writes:

> In all of the drafts of this play I have been obsessed with naming. What do we call ourselves as lesbians and Black women? How did we get our names? How do we assert our names? What are our past names? Each of the characters tells the story of her name. She is also searching for another name. She is in flux, reassessing her identity, travelling back into memory and forward into possibility. In order to change we have to examine who we say we are and how much of that has been imposed.[36]

At the very beginning of the play, the introduction of the "past," which is embedded in the story of each matrimonial name manifests the relationship between the individual and the community. In parallel to this, as Nira

32 Ibid., 64.

33 Ibid., 64–65.

34 Ibid., 82.

35 Collins Dictionary describes chiaroscuro as the use of light and shade in a picture, or the effect produced by light and shade in a place.

36 Lynette Goddard, *Staging Black Feminisms: Identity, Politics, Performance* (London: Palgrave Macmillan, 2007), 110.

Yuval-Davis points out, women are positioned as the "cultural carriers" of the ethnic group, particularly to the new generation.[37] Accordingly here, the names of women appear as the markers and maintainers of cultural heritage, though with its nonlinear lineage and ruptures. Significantly, by means of the passing down of familial names for generations, each name interlocks individual space and collective space as well as past and present. This act of intertwining might potentially reveal the latent intersecting values. In the case of Beth, it is significant to note that her grandmother was renamed under the oppressive regime of exploitation and slavery. In addition to the usurpation of her name/identity/culture, her body was also commodified as an object of desire and production in the service of the colonizer. The hegemonic Western discourse holds the privilege of naming the world and "others." In doing so, they assert dominance over individuals who refuse to agree with their set of norms. As Ashcroft argues, the act of naming "becomes a primary colonising process because it appropriates, defines, and captures the place in language."[38] Power's hold on race and sex is achieved and sustained through language. As to Yomi's grandmother, she is stripped of her voice and tries to transmit cultural values through drawing and painting. Metaphorically speaking, this situation alludes to women being retreated into silence in the face of subordination and abuse they confront. As seen in the case of both women, the discursive sphere of "otherized" people is taken control over and they are reduced into an object of control. As such, the exploration for identity gets more complicated when identity is "fractured by a non-linear relation to one's history."[39]

Throughout the play, each character takes her personal object from the chest that stays in the middle of the stage and proceeds to tell the story revolving around the particular object. All of these props take them to their childhood memories which are connected to the present in different ways. Aisha's personal object is a cushion on which she used to sit and listen to the stories her grandmother told her when she was a child. Aisha yearns for the memories the "magic" cushion reminds her of.[40] She reluctantly puts the cushion back into the chest saying "I didn't really know what she [grandmother] was on about then.

37 Floya, Anthias and Nira Yuval-Davis, "Introduction," in Woman-Nation-State, *edited by Nira Yuval-Davis and Floya Anthias* (London: Macmillan, 1989), 9.

38 Bill Ashcroft, Gareth Griffins, and Helen Tiffen, The Post-Colonial Studies Reader (New York and London: Routledge, 1995), 392.

39 Gabriele Griffin, Contemporary Black and Asian Women Playwrights in Britain (London: Cambridge University Press, 2003), 171.

40 Kay, *Chiaroscuro*, 66.

But I remembered it and now the words make sense. Good sense."[41] Opal gazes into an oval-shaped mirror through which her childhood trauma reactivates. Her reflection on the mirror agitates and haunts her:

> My face was a shock to itself. The brain in my head thought my skin White and my nose straight. It imagined my hair was this curly from twiddling it. Every so often, I saw me: milky coffee skin, dark searching eyes, flat nose. Some voice from that mirror would whisper: *nobody wants you, no wonder. You think you're White till you look in me. I surprised you, didn't I? I'd stop and will the glass to change me. Where did you get that nose?*[42]

A similar process of the internalized racial hatred operates in the case of Yomi. Yomi has a Black doll which she calls Amanda. When she was a small child, White kids were shouting at her: "Just because you're a darky doesn't mean you have to have a darky doll."[43] When she arrives at home, she puts the baby doll in the airing cupboard and projects her internalized racial hatred on the baby by reiterating derogatory insults of the White kids: "Nigger. Wog. Sambo. Dirty doll."[44] Yomi hugs the baby when she takes it from the chest and leaves it back by pitying it. Beth has a photograph album revealing that she had White boy friends and her mother is a White English woman. Although she is reluctant to show the album, Opal grabs it out of Beth's hands and reveals her past which seemingly she is eager to leave behind: "Sometimes I feel such a sham. When I was eighteen I rushed out and bought the Black records that had never sat on my selves, the blues, funk, jazz and soul I'd been missing. I bought books too. It was a whole new world. James Baldwin. Toni Morrison. C. L. R. James. I was excited."[45]

As the characters' emotional affiliation with their objects from the past conveys, the chest that contains the characters' personal props apparently represents the memory. These objects serve as a bridge between women and their past by triggering the act of remembering. Drawing upon Halbwachs's insights on the collective memory, March Bloch argues that remembering is an active process and reconstructs the past. He further states that "this reconstructive work is only possible because the individual mind has recourse to the group mind, which provides a framework for reconstructing the past."[46] Each time the

41 Ibid., 66.

42 Ibid., 78.

43 Ibid., 67.

44 Ibid., 67

45 Ibid., 96.

46 March Bloch, "From "Memoire Collective, Tradition et Coutume: A propos d'un Livre Recent," in The Collective Memory Reader, edited by Jeffrey K. Olick, Vered

women grab their objects initiates the act of revisiting past and memory, which accentuates the fact that "the individual consciousness" is not something "isolated and sealed within itself."[47] In other words, identity cannot be subsumed into one homogenous, stable or coherent category; on the contrary, it is negotiated and re-negotiated at the intersection of the particularities of time and space, and cultural legacy.[48] Indeed, the ways of remembering for the individual are undeniably conjectural. Power relations, conflicts, compromises in the present circumstances reconstruct collective memory.[49]

Their stories demonstrate that whiteness is represented not by the White characters on stage but by the lives of the Black female characters. The discourse, past, and desire of each character expose the domination of whiteness. The hegemonic structure and discourse of the whiteness set definite normative values regarding power relations. Each attempt these four women make to interact with their past is ruptured. Thus, their name stories and affiliation to their personal props signify that their history is also a long one of denial, silencing, and invisibility. The hierarchical dichotomy between White women and women of colour is also revealed. Peering into the mirror, Opal describes her body with offensive words such as "ugly features," "funny" and "pathetic."[50] She further states that "[m]y face is up like a big balloon. My eyes are swimming pools. My nose is an ape's nose. My lips are rubber. My face is dark and smooth. My cheeks are high and mellow."[51] Opal detests her physical appearance which does not fit the beauty standards fabricated by the Eurocentric discourse. As Debbie Weekes contends, "[w]hiteness and its associated outward signifiers have been used as a yardstick by which difference has been measured."[52] Internalizing the Western standards of female beauty, Opal looks at herself through the critical gaze of the

---

Vinitzky-Seroussi, and Daniel Levy, trans. by Jennifer Marie Silva (London: Oxford University Press, 2011), 151.

47 Maurice Halbwachs, "From *The Collective Memory*," in The Collective Memory Reader, edited by Jeffrey K. Olick, Vered Vinitzky-Seroussi, and Daniel Levy, trans. by Jennifer Marie Silva (London: Oxford University Press, 2011), 148.

48 Ibid., 148.

49 Jan Assmann, *Kültürel Bellek: Eski Yüksek Kültürlerde Yazı, Hatırlama ve Politik Kimlik*, trans. by Ayşe Tekin (İstanbul: Ayrıntı Yayınları, 1997), 44.

50 Kay, *Chiaroscuro*, 95–96.

51 Ibid., 100.

52 Debbie Weekes, "Shades of Blackness: Young Black Female Constructions of Beauty," in Black British Feminism: A Reader, *edited by Heidi Safia Mirza* (London and New York: Routledge, 1997), 114.

other. In a similar vein, Beth looks through the photo album and sees a photo in which she is wearing bobbles: "A little Black girl amongst the little White girls wearing bobbles in my hair, as if that would make me the same. I could never grow a ponytail."[53] In accordance with the Western standards of feminine beauty, whiteness is the most basic sign of the ideal beautiful woman. This assumption automatically excludes women of colour as the underprivileged leg of the binary opposition.[54] Thus, the Black woman realizes that "beauty" is unattainable for her as in the case of Opal and Beth. Turning Black women into "racialized"[55] bodies generates "hierarchies of femininity."[56] Body becomes the reference point through which racist discourse is maintained and reconstructed.[57] Nevertheless, the Black female body becomes a site through which women explore and construct their identity against the stereotypical assumptions about normative femininity.

The stories revolving around names and personal objects in the search of familial and cultural roots seem to contribute to the constitution of agency and subjectivity for the women, as resonated in Gayatri Spivak's essay "Can the Subaltern Speak?" Through identity narratives, the women tell how they and others see who they are. Martin shows how identity narrative gets also politicized: "it transforms the perception of the past and the present; it changes the organization of human groups and creates new ones; it alters cultures by emphasizing certain traits and skewing its meanings and logic; [it] brings forth a new interpretation of the world in order to modify it."[58] The reconstructing process of the past and the self through the name stories and personal objects opens up a discursive space for women. Remembering the history of colonization and cultural blockade as well as the immediate experiences of the present conditions of diaspora, women reclaim their names/identities from the domain

53 Kay, *Chiaroscuro*, 96.

54 Collins, *Black*, 194.

55 David Marriott, "The Racialized Body," in The Cambridge Companion to The Body in Literature, edited by David Hillman and Ulrika Maude (Cambridge: Cambridge University Press, 2015), 163. According to David Marriott, racist ideology produces "racialized body" as it signifies an identity belonging and operates as the "channel and point of transmission through which a racist notion of humanity is inherited and passed down" (2015, 163).

56 Collins, *Black*, 195.

57 Marriott, "The Racialized Body," 163.

58 Martin, Denis-Constant, "The Choices of Identity," Social Identities 1, no. 1 (1993): 13.

of the hegemonic Western ideology and discourse. More significantly, women continue to be the transmitters of the cultural legacy through identity narratives.

In the play, four women initially seem to unite around the shared experience of being marginalized in diaspora due to their skin colour, as implicated by their identical outfits at the beginning of the play. However, in the course of the events, other conflicts and hierarchies among them come to the fore. Towards the end of the second act, four women gather for dinner at Aisha and Yomi's flat. Opal is upset and talks about something that happened at the hospital that day: "I was telling one of my patients that it was curry for lunch" and she said, "It's not us that like that, but you coloured!" I didn't know what to say, so I just told her that I didn't like the word coloured, and she asked me what I'd call myself then. I told her Black. She laughed and said, "But you're a half-caste."[59] To Opal's frustration, Yomi advocates the use of "half-caste" for a person whose parents are of different races as it is the "reality." Outraged by this explanation, Beth strikes back:

Beth: It's derogatory – it's just like all those other horrible descriptions: half-breed, mulatto, the lot. It really gets to me when people insist on saying that I'm half and half.

Yomi: But it's true, isn't it?

Beth: What do you mean?

Yomi: Well, you are half and half; you can't just pretend that you don't have a White parent. You can't say that you're half White even if you don't …

Beth (*interrupting her*): Half White! […] Look, when I walk down the street and some NF thug wants to beat me up – what does he see, White or Black?

[…]

Yomi: He won't want to beat you up as much as he'd want to beat me up.[60]

Yomi further states that she pities people of mixed race as they are born into a complicated dilemma. Beth counter-argues that idea as she uses the word Black "as a political statement."[61] This scene reveals that there is no single practice of exclusion for women. While Opal is discriminated against as a Black woman by White people in the hospital, she is otherized by a Black woman for being a woman of mixed race. Afro-Caribbean women's domination over women of mixed race creates other hierarchies within the community. Thus, she is exposed to the practices of discrimination both in inter- and intra-communal facets. As the intersectional theory suggests, experiences can change in accordance with

59 Kay, *Chiaroscuro*, 88.

60 Ibid., 88–90.

61 Ibid., 90.

the identity belonging that comes to the fore within the particularities of time and space.

Furthermore, the opposite attitudes Beth and Opal embrace are also worth noting. It is seen that when compared to other women, Beth is seemingly a queer feminist and has political tendencies. Unlike Opal, she reacts sharply to the offensive remarks of Yomi. Obviously, Beth's experience as a woman of mixed race differs from the experience of another woman of mixed race, Opal, since Beth's political identity is also articulated to her other identity belongings. Therefore, each of the other identities added to womanhood diversifies experiences. From this perspective, there cannot be a single Black woman experience. Those who are discriminated against, as well as those who cause discrimination, cannot be subsumed into one homogenized category.

The conflict arising from the hierarchies among Black women deepens with the argument of homosexuality. Through the songs in the play, the reader/audience learns that it was really painful both for Opal and Beth to "come out of the closet" in their early ages. Moreover, Aisha also reveals to the reader/audience her lesbianism and describes the unpleasant feeling of smelling a man she does not like. However, she does not prefer to share it with her friends. When Yomi realizes that Beth and Opal are having a lesbian relationship which she calls "unnatural," she severely reacts: "Was I shocked! I felt so naïve. I've never seen two women kissing before. Long ones! Honestly! If they want to do that sort of thing they should do it behind closed doors. And Black women at that! I didn't think we produced them."[62] Apparently, the cause of inequalities does not only rely on blackness. When womanhood, lesbianism, politics are added as identity belongings, the forms of domination and the practices of discrimination deepen in diverse ways. Being Black, being a Black woman, and being a Black lesbian are the intersecting identities in the play and generates different disadvantaged positioning. Cultural and sexual hegemony are not only grounded in the dichotomy between whiteness and blackness. Ultimately, surpassing womanhood and blackness, sexual orientation has become the main motivation of the exclusionary practice. Heterosexism corresponds to another hegemonic order. Normative Black heterosexuality is constructed against Black queer identities by assuming an ideological role of the dominant cultural and religious values. In this scene, Yomi seems to idealize heterosexuality and demonize homosexuality. Thus, she establishes a symbiotic relationship between blackness and heterosexuality, both of which she idealizes. In fact, this also indicates that she establishes a

62 Ibid., 75–76.

pejorative association between whiteness and homosexuality. This instance also yields to intra-communal hierarchies on the grounds of sexual orientation. The subjugation of queer identities is multiplied by the intersection of discriminatory and intolerant acts as a form of microaggression. In this case, discriminatory practices are directed from the privileged leg of the opposition to the disadvantaged one within the Black community where heterosexuality retains its status as a cultural identifier.

At the end of the play, significantly women exchange their personal objects. Opal gives her photo album to Aisha who cannot come out of the closet so that she can break away with the "pretence" and liberate her sexual identity. Aisha offers her cushion to Opal who suffers from a lack of rootedness so that she can form a bond with the cultural history and come to grips with her bodily features. Opal gives her mirror to Yomi who holds racially and sexually prejudiced views so that she can confront her own bigotry. Finally, Yomi hands over her Black doll to Beth who wants to have a baby so that she can appreciate differences among women of colour. Rather than giving a romantic portrayal of Black sisterhood, Kay shows that "(re)inventing and (re)naming Black womanhood comes with recognition of both the similarities and the differences between them."[63] In a similar vein, Barney Bardsley puts that "[d]iscarding the superficial notion of harmonious sisterhood, Jackie Kay examines the complexities and contradictions of each woman – how she moves with and against her friends; how she comes to terms with her race, her sexuality, her history and her destiny."[64] Recognizing their peculiar experiences at the intersection of different identities opens up a discursive space for the characters to confront, negotiate and empathize with one another. At the end of the play, the exchange of special props might be an example for this promising note. They become aware of their different identities that conflict with each other. The play ends with a circular plot, which might signify the fact that identities will be in constant flux.

Conclusion

Over the last two decades, the concept of intersectionality has become a much-discussed issue within the feminist literature. Originally introduced and framed by Black feminists to render the exploitation of women of colour at the intersection of race and gender visible, the term has expanded to cover multiple

63 Goddard, *Staging*, 111.

64 Ibid., 111.

and diverse forms of domination and discriminatory practices to which under-represented and marginalized groups of women are subjected. The debate has principally been grounded on two argumentations. Firstly, "women oppression" cannot be isolated from other forms of oppression which are discursively and relationally established through diverse interlocking and reciprocally constructing intersections. There are multiple forms of exploitation and subjugation that arise from the articulation of race, class and gender-based identity categories. Secondly, the intersectional approach has posed a serious challenge to the Eurocentric, White and middle-class feminist discourse which assumes a universal and monolithic category of "women" who are subjected to "the same forms of oppression," regardless of racial or ethnic differences. The argument is that the intersectional approach can be used as an analytical tool to decipher strategies of power and discriminatory practices overlapping in the exclusion of women. In this regard, an intersectional approach helps comprehend the complexity of the dynamic and polyvalent processes and operations of power relations as multifaceted hierarchies manifest at the intersection of multiple and diverse identity belongings.

From the perspective of the intersectional feminist approach, this chapter has primarily concentrated on the multidimensional forms of domination and practices of discrimination that emerge at the intersection of different axes of identity belongings, with particular attention to Jackie Kay's political play *Chiaroscuro*. The play revolves around the stories of four Black women who dig into the recesses of their memory/past to remember, confront and redefine their selves informed by the intertwining and mutually constructing parameters. Their different positionings in terms of race, womanhood, lesbianism and political stance generate both inter- and intra-communal marginalization in diverse ways. In the play, women's recounting their identity narratives reconstructs the self who is situated at the crossroads of overlapping identity belongings informed by geography, ethnicity, the mediation of cultural production and the immediate experiences in the diaspora.

The chapter has critically investigated four Black women's stories to decipher the complicated mechanisms of power and oppression which lead to unique experiences and particular subjectivities. While doing this, the study also calls into question the tenets of mainstream feminism which assumes homogeneity of woman experience. Universalizing category of women perpetuated by White heterosexual Eurocentric feminism seems to be dysfunctional in addressing the difficulties Black women face on the grounds of the racialized and gendered exclusion. Furthermore, it is also obvious that a unitary Black identity or a monolithic voice for the whole community creates other hierarchies in itself.

As revealed in the case of Yomi, racist and sexist discourse is also intra-communally produced among Black women. As such, Black women are exposed to multi-layered forms of conflicts with the hegemonic Western discourse as well as intra-communal struggles.

Jackie Kay's concern in her work is to give voice to the voiceless and the marginalized. In parallel to this, as the intersectional approach aims to render invisible visible, it has provided a fruitful methodological tool to decipher the multidimensionality of domination and the practices of discrimination in Kay's play. Despite pointing at the never-ending conflicts with its circular ending, it will not be naïve to claim that the play ends on an optimistic note. By means of identity narratives and the exchange of the props, Kay presents the possibilities of dialogue and re-negotiation, if not a complete reconciliation, for women with one another and themselves when they recognize and appreciate their differences.

Bibliography

Ashcroft, Bill, Gareth Griffins, and Helen Tiffen. *The Post-Colonial Studies Reader*. New York and London: Routledge, 1995.

Assmann, Jan. *Kültürel Bellek: Eski Yüksek Kültürlerde Yazı, Hatırlama ve Politik Kimlik*. İstanbul: Ayrıntı Yayınları, 1997.

Beal, Frances. "Double Jeopardy: To Be Black and Female." In *The Black Woman*, edited by Toni Cade Bambara, 90–100. New York: Signet, 1970.

Billington, Michael. "*Chiaroscuro* Review – Jackie Kay's Play is More Gig than Theatre." *The Guardian*, 2019.

Bloch, March. "From 'Memoire Collective, Tradition et Coutume: A Propos d'un Livre Recent.'" In *The Collective Memory Reader*, edited by Jeffrey K. Olick, Vered Vinitzky-Seroussi, and Daniel Levy, translated by Jennifer Marie Silva, 150–155. London: Oxford University Press, 2011.

Brooks, Libby. "Don't tell me who I am." *The Guardian*. 12 January 2002. https://www.theguardian.com/books/2002/jan/12/fiction.features

Butler, Judith. *Gender Trouble: Feminism and the Subversion of Identity*. London: Routledge, 1999.

Carastathis, Anna. "The Concept of Intersectionality in Feminist Theory." *Philosophy Compass* 9, no. 5 (2014): 304–314.

Collins, Patricia Hill. *Black Feminist Thought: Knowledge, Consciousness, and the Politics of Empowerment*. 2nd ed. New York and London: Routledge, 2000.

Collins, Patricia Hill. *Black Sexual Politics: African Americans, Gender, and the New Racism*. New York and London: Routledge, 2004.

Collins, Patricia Hill and Sırma Bilge. *Intersectionality*. 2nd ed. Cambridge: Polity Press, 2020.

Crenshaw, Kimberlé. "Demarginalizing the Intersection of Race and Sex: A Black Feminist Critique of Antidiscrimination Doctrine, Feminist Theory and Antiracist Politics." *University of Chicago Legal Forum* 1, article 8 (1989). https://chicagounbound.uchicago.edu/uclf/vol1989/iss1/8

Crenshaw, Kimberlé. "Mapping the Margins: Intersectionality, Identity Politics, and Violence against Women of Color." *Stanford Law Review* 43, no. 6 (1991): 1241–1299.

Crenshaw, Kimberlé, "The Urgency of Intersectionality." *TEDWomen*, 2016. https://www.ted.com/talks/kimberle_crenshaw_the_urgency_of_intersectionality?language=en#t-294596

Crenshaw, Kimberlé. "Kesişimsellik Hemen Şimdi!" *5Harfliler*, 2017. http://www.5harfliler.com/kesisimsellik-hemen-simdi/

Davis, Angela. "The Personal is Political: Gendered Identities in the Twenty-First Century." *The Eight Biennial Associated Colleges of the South Gender Studies Conference*, Rhodes College and the Gender and Sexuality Studies Department, 6–7 Mart 2009.

Davis, Kathy. "Intersectionality as Buzzword: A Sociology of Science Perspective on What Makes a Feminist Theory Successful." *Feminist Theory* 9, no. 1, (2008): 67–85.

Floya, Anthias and Nira Yuval-Davis, "Introduction." In *Woman-Nation-State*, edited by Nira Yuval-Davis and Floya Anthias, 1–15. London: Macmillan, 1989.

Fraser, Nancy. "Pragmatism, Feminism, and the Linguistic Turn." In *Feminist Contentions: A Philosophical Exchange*, edited by Seyla Benhabib et al., 157–171. New York and London: Routledge, 1995.

Griffin, Gabriele. *Contemporary Black and Asian Women Playwrights in Britain*. London: Cambridge University Press, 2003.

Goddard, Lynette. *Staging Black Feminisms: Identity, Politics, Performance*. London: Palgrave Macmillan, 2007.

Halbwachs, Maurice. "From *The Collective Memory*." In *The Collective Memory Reader*, edited by Jeffrey K. Olick, Vered Vinitzky-Seroussi, and Daniel Levy, translated by Jennifer Marie Silva, 139–149. London: Oxford University Press, 2011.

Innes, C. L. "Accent and Identity: Women Poets of Many Parts." In *Contemporary British Poetry: Essays in Theory and Criticism*, edited by James Acheson and Romana Huk, 315–341. New York: State University of New York Press, 1996.

Kay, Jackie. "An Interview with Jackie Kay." *The Children's Poetry Archive*, 2005. https://childrens.poetryarchive.org/interviews/an-interview-with-jackie-kay/

Kay, Jackie. *Chiaroscuro*. In *The Methuen Drama Book of Plays by Black British Writers*. London: Bloomsbury, 2011.

King, Deborah. "Multiple Jeopardy, Multiple Consciousness: The Concept of a Black Feminist Ideology." *Signs* 14, no. 1, (1988): 42–72.

Kirkness, Verna. "Emerging Native Women." *Canadian Journal of Women and Law* 2, (1987–1988): 408–415.

Marriott, David. "The Racialized Body." In *The Cambridge Companion to The Body in Literature*, edited by David Hillman and Ulrika Maude, 163–176. Cambridge: Cambridge University Press, 2015.

Martin, Denis-Constant. "The Choices of Identity." *Social Identities* 1, no. 1 (1993): 5–20.

McCall, Leslie. "The Complexity of Intersectionality." *Signs* 30, no. 3 (2005): 1771–1800.

Sierz, Aleks. *Rewriting the Nation: British Theatre Today*. London: Methuen, 2011.

Sigle-Rushton, Wendy and Elin Lindström. "Intersectionality." In *Gender: The Key Concepts*, edited by Mary Evans and Carolyn Williams, 129–134. New York and London: Routledge, 2013.

Staunæs, Dorthe. "Where Have All the Subjects Gone? Bringing Together the Concepts of Intersectionality and Subjectification." *NORA – Nordic Journal of Feminist and Gender Research* 11, no. 2 (2003): 101–110.

Weekes, Debbie. "Shades of Blackness: Young Black Female Constructions of Beauty." In *Black British Feminism: A Reader*, edited by Heidi Safia Mirza, 113–126. London and New York: Routledge, 1997.

West, Cornel. "The New Cultural Politics of Difference." In *The Postmodern Turn: New Perspectives on Social Theory*, edited by Steven Seidman, 65–81. Cambridge: Cambridge University Press, 1994.

Yuval-Davis, Nira. *The Politics of Belonging: Intersectional Contestations*. London: Sage, 2011.

Notes on Contributors

Gökçe Akarik (Lecturer) is currently working at Cağ University in Turkey. She completed her MA degree under the supervision of Dr Enes Kavak in English Literature at Gaziantep University in Turkey. Her thesis was titled "Temporality and Spatiality in Contemporary British Theatre."

Mustafa Bal (Assistant Professor of English Literature), holding BA, MA (Hacettepe University) and PhD (Middle East Technical University) degrees in English Language and Literature, currently works as an assistant professor and the chair of the Department of English Language and Literature at TOBB University of Economics and Technology in Turkey. His studies concentrate especially on the contemporary British drama that encompasses the period from the post-war era to the present. Mustafa Bal is also a translator who, apart from his short translations from Virginia Woolf, T.S. Eliot, Gogol, and Bernard Shaw, translated James Joyce's *Dubliners*, Seamus Heaney's *North* (the first translation of a collection by the poet to Turkish), and George Orwell's *Nineteen Eighty-Four* and *Animal Farm* to Turkish.

Mehmet Akif Balkaya (Assistant Professor of English Literature) completed his undergraduate degree in English Language and Literature at Cumhuriyet University and his master's and doctorate degrees in English Culture and Literature at Atılım University in Turkey. He has published articles and books on Shakespeare, James Joyce, nineteenth-century industrial novels and literary theories. He is currently a full-time faculty at Necmettin Erbakan University in Turkey.

Pelin Doğan (Assistant Professor of English Literature) received her bachelor's degree from the Department of English Language and Literature at Gaziantep University, Turkey, in 2010. She received her PhD from the Department of English Language and Literature at Ankara University in 2017, with a thesis titled "Censorship in Twentieth and Twenty-First Century British Drama: Representations and Responses." Currently, she works as an assistant professor at Munzur University, Department of English Language and Literature. Her fields of interest include contemporary British theatre, censorship in early and contemporary British theatre and gender studies.

Hakan Gültekin (Assistant Professor of English Literature) is a faculty member at Artvin Coruh University Department of English Language and Literature in Turkey. He received his MA degree from Karadeniz Technical University in 2014. He completed his PhD in the English Literature Department of İstanbul Aydın University. In his research, he focuses on American and British short stories, contemporary British drama and literary theory. His dissertations examined writers such as Ernest Hemingway, David Hare, Howard Barker, Mark Ravenhill and Lucy Kirkwood.

Mesut Günenç (Assistant Professor of English Literature) got his BA and MA at Ataturk University/Erzurum and completed a PhD on Postdramatic Theatre in English literature. He is currently teaching at Aydın Adnan Menderes University. He has published articles, especially on Contemporary British Drama in national and international journals. He has published book chapters titled "Passions of William Shakespeare's Lesser-Known Characters: Tim Crouch I, Shakespeare" and "Victimized Woman: Sarah Kane's Phaedra's Love" and a book titled *David Hare'in Oyunlarında Post-Truth Söylem* in 2019. He has also received a TUBITAK research scholarship and will be visiting Loughborough University for his post-PhD studies in 2022. He is a founding member of Theatre and Drama Network (TDN) in Turkey.

Özlem Karadağ (Assistant Professor of English Literature) teaches in the English Department at Istanbul University, specializing in theatre studies and trauma narratives along with poetry, literary adaptations and contemporary literary theories. She received her BA (2005), MA (2008), and PhD (2013) degrees from Istanbul University's English Language and Literature Department and took a postdoctoral position at Queen Mary University of London, Department of Drama (2015), where she had also conducted her PhD research in 2012. In 2012, she also joined BuluTiyatro as a resident dramaturg and has also translated many contemporary English plays. Some of her recent publications include *Ecofeminist Ecopoetics and Carol Ann Duffy* and *Unreal City: The Image of the City in T. S. Eliot's Poetry* and two articles in Turkish titled "The Revenge of Nature?: Nature Taking Over Civilization in Thomas Eccleshare's *Pastoral*" in *Navisalvia: Natura* and "Text and Performance as an Interdisciplinary and Intermedia Rewriting: Hamletmachine (1977) and 'Death Suits Ophelia' (2005)" in *Studien zur deutschen Sprache und Literatur*.

Enes Kavak (Assistant Professor of English Literature) is currently working as an assistant professor at Gaziantep University. He holds a PhD in English Literature from the University of Leeds, the United Kingdom. His doctoral research titled "Spectacle, Performance and New Femininities in the Plays of Suffrage Playwrights between 1907 and 1914" focuses on Edwardian women's political theatre. He is the co-editor of an edited volume titled *English Studies in the 21st Century* and has published articles and book chapters on British suffrage theatre and contemporary British playwright Howard Barker. His recent research focuses mostly on suffrage literature, women's writings, contemporary drama and theatre. He is a founding member of Theatre and Drama Network (TDN) in Turkey.

Gül Kurtuluş (Lecturer of English Literature) is currently a lecturer at the English Language and Literature Department of Bilkent University in Turkey. She received her PhD in English literature from the same university in 1997. Her major research and teaching interest is English drama and theatre. She has published various articles on drama and her first monograph, titled *Stereoscopic London: Plays of Oscar Wilde, Bernard Shaw and Arthur Wing Pinero in the 1890s*, was published by Peter Lang in 2020.

www.ingramcontent.com/pod-product-compliance
Lightning Source LLC
Chambersburg PA
CBHW060756310726
48980CB00002B/115

9783631860229